RESPONDING TO INFANTS

RESPONDING TO INFANTS

THE INFANT ACTIVITY MANUAL
6 to 30 Months

Developed through the auspices of Respond, Inc.,
Day Care Centers of Camden, New Jersey,
and authored by Inez D. Moyer, Curriculum Coordinator

Publishers
T.S. Denison and Company, Inc.
Minneapolis

Publishers
SINCE 1876

T.S. Denison & Company, Inc.

Standard Book Number: 513-01769-0
Library of Congress Card Number: 83-71345
Copyright © 1983 by T.S. Denison & Co., Inc.
Minneapolis, Minnesota 55431
Printed in the USA

CONTENTS

PREFACE

This curriculum manual was written in response to a need for a practical, useful guide to activities to use with infants of ages six months to thirty months. The activities are easy, inexpensive, and don't require complicated equipment, yet they meet the baby's individual developmental needs. This is a *working* manual that can be easily used without lengthy searching for appropriate activities. Therefore, parents and day care and nursery school workers will find this manual a valuable aid in helping their children get off to a good start in life. Students in early childhood education and pediatric fields will also find it a practical guide to help them as they deal with very young children.

In order to make this manual easy to use, the curriculum has been divided into six major areas. These are: *Fine Motor, Gross Motor, Intellectual, Social/Emotional, Language,* and *Self-Care.* A chart of developmental levels for each area is included, describing behaviors at each level. These are keyed numerically to many activity suggestions for working with the child at his own level.

It should be stressed that the use of chronological age in the developmental charts is only for convenience. We wish to emphasize that the child's behavior and abilities are the important criteria in determining his level of development. Some children will be ahead of the age range in some areas, while some may be behind the age range. It is important to remember that the actual age of the child is the least important fact of his individual development.

You will notice that in most cases throughout the manual, we speak about the baby and the activities you can do with him using the singular "baby" rather that the plural "babies." We did this to help emphasize the fact that each child is an individual. We hope that this will help you to look upon each baby as an independent and important person all by himself. Of course, all of these activities are intended for use with all babies, when they reach the indicated levels of development.

You will also notice that we use the masculine gender, for the most part, when referring to the baby. This too, is done for convenience and simplicity, since we know that you all are working with both girls and boys. It is just too cumbersome to keep saying "he or she," etc.

Safety cannot be stressed too much when working with babies and young children. Always be sure that all materials you buy or make to use with the baby cannot hurt him, or let him hurt himself in any way. Look over articles you plan to give to the baby carefully. Some articles can't be used by the baby unless you plan to stay with him and watch him while he uses it. Make your motto "Safety First."

HOW TO USE THIS MANUAL

This curriculum is divided into six major areas. They are:
    Fine Motor
    Gross Motor
    Intellectual
    Social/Emotional
    Language
    Self-Care

Each area has been divided into four developmental age levels. They are:
    6—12 months
    12—18 months
    18—24 months
    24—30 months

If, for instance, the child you are working with has begun to notice and be interested in his nose or his toes, look at the developmental chart, under "Intellectual," #77. You'll see that the baby should soon learn to point to his body parts when you ask him to. To help him learn to do this, turn to the same section in the activities portion, and there you will find under #77 a group of activities that you can use with him.

This describes the way you should use the book for every area and every level in the developmental chart. Don't worry if the baby is not the exact age listed. These age divisions are for convenience in describing development. The important thing to remember is that these activities will work best with the baby when he has reached the stage of development where *he* is ready for the next step.

We would like to thank Florence Gillespie, Center Coordinator, and her staff during the writing of this manual. They are Lillian Syms, Rubbie Jordan, Mae Wilson, Carmen Santiago, Mary Brown, Janet Lark, and Margaret Woods. Their help and support was much appreciated. Sadly, we cannot thank Beatrice Murray, Director, Infant Center, for all her help in compiling this manual. She died on April 13, 1978, while the manual was still in process. Her loss is deeply felt by all of us at Respond, Inc.

Much appreciation is also extended to Mr. Wilbert Mitchell, our Executive Director, and the staffs of our five other Day Care Centers for their support, understanding and help.

Many, many thanks goes to our competent and cooperative typist, Evelyne Benjamin, who so willingly and patiently transcribed all of this material.

DEDICATED TO THE MEMORY
OF
MRS. BEATRICE MURRAY

SUPERVISOR
OF
RESPOND, INC.—INFANT CENTER
October, 1971 to April, 1978

ACKNOWLEDGEMENTS

The materials listed below are from the books *From Birth to One Year* by Marilyn M. Segal, Ph.D., © Nova University, 1974, and *From One to Two Years* by Marilyn Segal and Don Adcock, © Nova University, 1976.

For permission to use these materials, grateful acknowledgement is made to B.L. Winch and Associates, Publishers, 45 Hitching Post Drive, Bldg. (2), Rolling Hills Estates, California 90274

From Birth to One Year

Toys:

- *Merry-Go-Round Mobile*
- *Wrist Bands*
- *Finger Glove*
- *Shadow Box*
- *Finger Puppet*
- *Funny Foot Sock*
- *Rag Doll*
- *Happy-Sad Pillow*
- *Happy-Sad Plate Puppet*
- *Bean Bag Face Puppet*
- *Paper Bag Puppet*
- *Jingle-Jangle Fish*
- *"Pat" Picture Book*
- *Mitten Puppet*
- *Squeak Book*
- *Tote Bag*
- *Paper Plate Puppet*

Rhymes:

- *Little Bird, Little Bird, Fly About*
- *Chug-Chug-Chug-Chug*
- *Up My Little Bundle Comes*
- *Where Is Baby's Nose?*
- *Good Morning, Mr. Thumb-0*
- *Up-Up-Up My Baby Goes*
- *Clap Your Hands, One-Two-Three*
- *Up My Arms Go*
- *We Roll The Ball*

From One to Two Years

Toys:

- *Finger Puppet*
- *Cradle*
- *Guess the Picture Book*
- *Painted Spool Matching Game*

As the baby grows, he will . . .	And so the baby needs . . .	You can help the baby learn if you . . .	Look at Activity #
look all around at things, near and far	interesting objects, people, etc., to look at	move around, try to catch baby's attention	1
hold onto objects, look at them, put them in his mouth	many and varied articles to play with and hold	give baby safe objects with interesting shapes that he can easily hold	2
spend time looking at his own hands	time and freedom to do this	move mobiles and other objects further away; let baby look at his hands	3
bring his hands in front of his body and hold them together	opportunity and encouragement to practice this new skill	hold small, safe objects in front of baby so he can grab for them with both hands	4
turn his body and grab an object with both hands	to practice these coordinating skills	let baby play with objects that he must turn toward and reach out for	5
be able to hold two toys at once, reaching across his body to get the second toy	to practice grabbing one object as he holds another	play toy-passing games using only two toys; extend a toy to the hand that already has a toy	6
learn about things by handling them—his eyes and hands are learning to work together	to discover the size, shape, weight, feel of things for himself	give him many interesting things to look at and explore	7

FINE MOTOR, 6—12 MONTHS

As the baby grows, he will . . .	And so the baby needs . . .	You can help the baby learn if you . . .	Look at Activity #
begin to use a thumb and fore-finger grip (pincher grip)	opportunity to pick up small items from a flat surface	show baby how to pick up these items; finger foods give baby a reward for practicing	8
begin to poke, pat, etc. and to discover that things stay where they are even when he can't see them	to discover object permanence, and learn about hollow and solid, inside and outside, up and down, etc.	give baby toys that will help him learn these things	9
let you keep a toy for him while he's playing with other toys	you to play at keeping a toy safe for him	play at passing toys back and forth with baby; see how many he can hold	10
enjoy playing with all kinds of objects	to be given a large variety of articles to play with	give baby things he can use easily, such as baskets, hats, and things that fit inside each other	11
use different actions with different objects	practice with various objects that can be used in different ways	demonstrate how to use things; try crumpling paper, pulling a toy, squeezing a toy to make it squeak, etc.	12
drop or throw objects	opportunity to practice a new skill: "cast and release"	start baby in a cycle of dropping or throwing a ball or a cardboard tube; keep handing it back; back and forth ball-rolling is another "cycle" game	13
like to play with many things, dropping one and picking up another, one by one	opportunities to practice this, since this one-by-one action is a developmental prerequisite for learning to count	show baby how to pick things up and drop them one by one	14

As the baby grows, he will . . .	And so the baby needs . . .	You can help the baby learn if you . . .	Look at Activity #
put his spoon into his cup and let go of it; hold his cup with both hands and drink from it	spoons and cups to practice with	show baby how to do this; then let him try	15

FINE MOTOR, 12—18 MONTHS

As the baby grows, he will . . .	And so the baby needs . . .	You can help the baby learn if you . . .	Look at Activity #
hold his cup with both hands and drink from it	opportunity to practice with a filled cup	let baby practice this skill that must be learned; expect spills	16
try to put one 2″ block on top of another of the same size	to be given blocks of this size to play with	show baby what kinds of things he can do with blocks	17
scribble on a large sheet of paper, while holding his crayon in his fist	paper and brightly colored crayons to use	let baby do his own thing with the color of his choice on a large sheet of paper	18
begin to turn pages in large stiff-paged books	books that are colorful and attractive to him	sit down with baby and a book; let him try to turn pages; be patient	19
like to run around, but will sit still for awhile to play with interesting objects	many interesting objects to help his eye-hand coordination, and to give him a quiet time	realize that this is a very active age, but try to interest baby in sitting and handling small objects	20

FINE MOTOR, 18—24 MONTHS

As the baby grows, he will . . .	And so the baby needs . . .	You can help the baby learn if you . . .	Look at Activity #
unscrew loose lid on jar	practice with large jars (plastic) that have lids that screw on	show him how to take the jar lid off and then put it on; let him practice	21
imitate a vertical stroke on paper	much practice with paper and crayon before he can do this	try making various single crayon strokes; see if he tries to imitate your strokes even slightly	22
connect and disconnect large popette beads	supervised play with popette beads (be sure they are too big to swallow)	let him have lots of practice in trying to connect and disconnect beads; demonstrate how; let him try other ways to hook things together	23
try to refine his fine motor skills	many manipulative toys and experiences to practice new fine motor skills	encourage baby as he refines his fine motor skills; praise him for the things he does	24
look at magazines, (and tear them up)	books that can be easily torn	give him magazines that he can tear up	25
remove his hat and mittens, snap large snaps, and unzip a large zipper	opportunity to do as much for himself as possible—be patient	show baby how to do these things, and then encourage him to do them for himself	26
correctly place circles and squares in a form board	many manipulative experiences	demonstrate, then let baby play with manipulatory puzzles (large, few pieces) and toys	27

As the baby grows, he will . . .	And so the baby needs . . .	You can help the baby learn if you . . .	Look at Activity #
roll, pound, and squeeze clay	opportunities to play with clay, play-dough, sand, etc.	let the child make what he wants to with these materials; don't make models for him to copy	28
string beads together	opportunities to play with large beads and other items to string	make sure beads, etc. are too large to swallow	29
turn pages of book singly	interesting books and magazines	look at books often; let him turn the pages; get him interested in the pictures	30

FINE MOTOR, 24—30 MONTHS

fold paper when he sees you fold paper	much practice with folding and tearing paper	demonstrate how to fold paper; let the child try; let him discover many ways to fold paper	31
nest four or more small square boxes	many boxes and other containers to play with	demonstrate how to nest boxes and then let the child try it; encourage him to do it his way, even if it is not quite right	32
draw a crude circle	many opportunities to use crayon and paper	have him use as large a piece of paper as possible; encourage and praise his efforts	33

FINE MOTOR, 24—30 MONTHS

As the baby grows, he will . . .	And so the baby needs . . .	You can help the baby learn if you . . .	Look at Activity #
use alternate hands and twist forearm, (but cannot turn doorknob)	more opportunities and more freedom to manipulate objects	supply many and varied articles and toys for baby to play with	34
fit things into one another (likes to take things apart and put them together)	objects that can be taken apart and put together again	give baby toys that give him problems to solve; make sure all objects are safe for baby to play with	35

GROSS MOTOR, 0 - 12 MONTHS

As the baby grows, he will . . .	And so the baby needs . . .	You can help the baby learn if you . . .	Look at Activity #
actively move arms and legs	activities and objects to stimulate movement	change baby's position many times, from back to stomach; place objects (rattle, large plastic ring, etc.) in his hand	36
turn body towards object	opportunities to perform directed body turns	try to get the infant to adjust his body to the movement of the object you are holding so he can see it	37
gradually gain control of back muscles—sit up, with support	opportunities to practice sitting up	play exercise games while you hold his hands	38
try hitting (with up and down arm movement) and shaking (side to side arm movement)	many objects and toys, so he can practice these movements	demonstrate hitting an object against a hard surface, and then pat the surface with your hand; encourage baby to copy you	39
bounce his body in a rhythmic manner	to become used to gentle swaying and other rhythmic movements as he is held in caregiver's arms	bounce him on your knees, while music is in the background to set the tempo	40
sit without support	practice in controlling things around him by using his body	place attractive toys near him, but so that he must reach for them	41
perform much gross motor activity	opportunity to practice these new motor skills	see that he has many interesting objects and people to interact with	42

GROSS MOTOR, 6—12 MONTHS

As the baby grows, he will . . .	And so the baby needs . . .	You can help the baby learn if you . . .	Look at Activity #
crawl to get from one place to another	plenty of opportunity to practice moving around, and to learn to make body fit into the space available	place baby on a clean rug or blanket that will not move under him, creating a safe, attractive area for him to move in	43
pull himself upright, and stand firmly while holding on	opportunities to move around and practice beginning walking	encourage him to walk, while giving him strong help and support; if he seems reluctant or frightened, stop and try again another time	44
crawl up and down steps	opportunity to practice this skill in a safe environment	help baby to begin his upward exploration by aiding and encouraging him to climb up onto low stools, etc.	45

GROSS MOTOR, 12—18 MONTHS

walk well unsupported	opportunities to practice walking, dancing, marching, running, etc.	provide pull toys to encourage the child to walk	46
move from sitting or stooping to standing position without help	opportunities to practice this and other gross motor activities	help baby to explore and use his very strong gross motor drive	47
develop casting or overhand throwing; these actions are very important developmental behavior patterns	much practice of these kinds of activities; this helps the child gain control of his body and his balance	give him toys that he can throw safely, especially balls, both large and small	48

GROSS MOTOR, 12—18 MONTHS

As the baby grows, he will . . .	And so the baby needs . . .	You can help the baby learn if you . . .	Look at Activity #
do much exploring; travel and carry objects from one place to another; be ceaselessly active	many opportunities to find and explore things in the environment	make a very rich environment for baby to explore, both indoors and outdoors	49
try out the many ways he can run, walk, etc.	constantly supervised opportunities to run freely	let him run and play very actively, but always maintain a safe and well supervised area for his play	50
pound large pegs into a workbench	opportunities to perform this	always supervise pounding or hammering activities; show baby how to do it, then let him try; stay with him as long as he is interested	51

GROSS MOTOR, 18—24 MONTHS

As the baby grows, he will . . .	And so the baby needs . . .	You can help the baby learn if you . . .	Look at Activity #
walk with more direction to his movements, and go to places knowingly and with remembrance	opportunities to find things, replace things, store things	play games that require baby to move in given directions and let him invent games; join in if he wants you to	52
kick a ball forward without losing balance, and throw a small ball forward	opportunities to kick and throw balls, both inside and outside	demonstrate how to kick and throw a ball; then let him try	53
walk up and down stairs alone, both feet on one step at a time and holding onto railing	opportunities to climb up and down stairs and other obstacles	schedule time for him to walk upstairs; be sure to accompany him, but don't take his hand unless he seems insecure or frightened.	54

GROSS MOTOR, 24—30 MONTHS

As the baby grows, he will . . .	And so the baby needs . . .	You can help the baby learn if you . . .	Look at Activity #
stand on either foot and balance; also jump and stand on tiptoes	much freedom and many opportunities to play and be physically active with feet and legs	show the child how to play games and to do things that will use his leg and foot muscles	55
walk between parallel lines approximately 8″ apart	opportunities to try out and learn this skill of balance	let the child do many activities designed to help him achieve balance	56
become very active and not sit still much; coordination is better now	lots of supervision yet; the child seems more mature, but don't be tempted to overestimate him	give the toddler "action" toys to play with, such as cars, climbing apparatus, push/pull toys, tricycles, wagons, swings, rocking-horses, or boats	57

As the baby grows, he will . . .	And so the baby needs . . .	You can help the baby learn if you . . .	Look at Activity #
turn his eyes toward the source of sounds	to be spoken to and to hear other noises from all areas of the room	provide baby with much interaction by calling to him, playing music, or making various noises to attract his attention	58
smile and talk to faces or objects, such as a mirror	much opportunity to interact with others	play "Peek-a-boo" games with baby, so that he can become familiar with them and learn to expect a series of actions	59
follow a moving object with his eyes, but will not look for an object that has disappeared	opportunities to observe objects that appear, disappear, reappear	place mobiles over his crib or playpen that are partially screened as they move	60
reject an object or toy after playing with it many times	a variety of toys and objects that are continually new and different to him	provide toys and objects that encourage handling and exploring for size, shape, color, texture, movement, position, and sound	61
watch a fast moving object as it goes up, down or sideways	moving objects to watch	play with baby by moving objects, including your face, for baby to follow	62
usually not turn objects over to see the other side	many interesting objects to play with	show baby an object, and then turn it over; let baby try to do it; then give him the object to play with	63
look carefully at an object set in front of him by picking it up and turning it in many ways	many odd shaped objects to play with and study	introduce baby to variety of objects with odd and interesting shapes and features	64

INTELLECTUAL, 6—12 MONTHS

As the baby grows, he will . . .	And so the baby needs . . .	You can help the baby learn if you . . .	Look at Activity #
be able to find and grab an object which moves after he begins to reach for it; he'll reach for toys out of his reach	moving objects to reach for and non-moving items that are placed just out of his reach	hold a small object in front of baby, and when he reaches for it, place it in back of something that will hide it; remove what hides it and let him reach for it	65
imitate you in doing "Patty Cake," hand-clapping and other simple movements such as shaking a bell or a rattle	people to interact with him and give him actions to imitate	play simple hand-clapping games with him, along with other simple motion games	66
be able to line up a cube in one hand with one in his other hand	blocks and cubes to play with	show him how to put cubes and other objects together in a line; encourage him to try	67
uncover a toy he has seen hidden	opportunities to watch and find things he sees disappear	show baby a favorite toy, then partly hide it under a blanket; see if he can uncover it and find it	68
search for a toy removed from his sight, but will always look in the place where it first disappeared	opportunity to practice searching for objects	hide an object, let baby find it, then try hiding it in a different place	69
repeat his actions if he gets people to laugh and play with him	much encouragement from his "audience" for him to perform	try not to overdo this, but help baby to be interested in continuing this kind of play and learning by much response to him	70
begin to see and handle things with more awareness (notices it is round or soft, etc.)	help in finding out that his environment is not flat	help him to become aware of the various qualities of objects, and to become aware of two as well as one	71

As the baby grows, he will . . .	And so the baby needs . . .	You can help the baby learn if you . . .	Look at Activity #
look at and point to pictures in a book	many books and magazines with large and colorful pictures	sit with him and talk to him about what he sees; encourage him to point out what he sees	72
find an object by looking in the right place when it is hidden in first one place, then another, and then a third place	still more opportunities to play seek and find	play hiding games with baby by hiding objects in several places; leave part of the object exposed so he can see it	73
understand and follow simple commands	much action with adult caregivers, on a "give and take" basis	give baby a group of toys, then ask him for one; if he doesn't cooperate, don't insist; try again later	74
find an object even if it is covered completely when hidden from him	more opportunities to find things that disappear	hide an object from the baby and then move it to another hiding place; see if he can find it when it is completely hidden	75
point to a specific object he wants, and "tell" you that he wants it	to learn the names of the many objects in his world	encourage baby to ask for things by answering his signals and helping him to learn the names of things	76
when asked, point to three body parts	help in learning the parts of his body	use the names of body parts when talking to the child during daily activities	77
place a circle and a square in the proper slots of a form board	much practice with various shapes	work patiently with him, showing him how various shapes are alike and how they are different	78

INTELLECTUAL, 12—18 MONTHS

As the baby grows, he will . . .	And so the baby needs . . .	You can help the baby learn if you . . .	Look at Activity #
give you several common objects when you ask for them by name	much practice in naming objects	tell baby the names of objects you and he are using, all during the day in every activity	79
look toward an object or place when told to "Look at . . ."	to know more about the directions and names of things	point out to baby all the things of interest in his environment, so that he becomes aware of them and where they are	80
point to a particular picture in a book when you name it (e.g. "Find the ball.")	to be given names for all the pictures he looks at	always name the objects you and he see in books or magazines that you look at together	81

INTELLECTUAL, 18—24 MONTHS

follow three simple directions, in order	to learn how to do things in a certain order, as he is asked	give baby simple directions, in order, so that he can easily follow them	82
refer to himself by his own name, and name other familiar objects	the opportunity to learn and use his own name and the names of objects	always use baby's own name when you talk to him, and name objects and toys that you and he use together during the day	83
be able to understand longer and harder sentences	opportunities to try to understand the meaning of longer and harder sentences	keep increasing the length of your sentences and conversations with baby, as long as he understands you	84

As the baby grows, he will . . .	And so the baby needs . . .	You can help the baby learn if you . . .	Look at Activity #
use a stick to reach a toy that is out of his reach	practice in learning this new skill	show baby how he can pull a toy toward himself with something other than his own hand	85
point to objects that match or are almost like a familiar sample	much practice in looking at and noticing details of objects	point out to baby what is the same and what is different about the objects he is using	86
understand the meaning of the word "another"	opportunities to respond to this word—this is beginning counting	use the word "another" whenever you can	87
be able to pick out his own coat and other belongings from everybody else's	practice in going to get the toys and other things that he wants or needs	let baby try to find what he wants for himself; this helps child learn	88

INTELLECTUAL, 24—30 MONTHS

be able to say what sex he or she is	the opportunity to find out whether he or she is a boy or a girl	refer to baby as a boy or girl, and discuss with the children that some of them are boys and some of them are girls	89
point to smaller body parts (nose, eyes, etc.) when asked	practice in learning the names of these various body parts	include these smaller body parts when you point out the child's body parts to him	90

INTELLECTUAL, 24—30 MONTHS

As the baby grows, he will . . .	And so the baby needs . . .	You can help the baby learn if you . . .	Look at Activity #
be able to match and compare familiar objects as to color, form, or size, and to group them in these ways	opportunities to handle objects so as to become aware of these ideas	help him to observe and notice how things compare with each other in regard to these ideas (as: which one is big and which one is small)	91
have a short attention span, but he will make up for it by repeating some activities and changing them a little	plenty of time to work with the toys and objects that interest him, for as long as they interest him	allow baby to determine for himself when he has had enough of an activity, and give him as much freedom of choice as possible	92
begin counting to two, and be aware of how many makes two; he may even be able to repeat two numbers in order	much practice in learning that one object and another object make two objects	ask the child to hand you one more of something; follow this by counting them and then asking him to count them	93
ask a question when he misunderstands what someone has said	response to his questions	always remember that the child deserves a good answer to his questions; be patient with him when he misunderstands	94
join in the singing of nursery rhymes and songs	to learn the words and tunes of all the nursery songs that you can find	make sure that you say the words clearly, and he understands what the actions mean	95
delight in pointing out all of the many small details in a picture	to look at more detailed pictures, with many more things in them for him to look at	look at these pictures with him, and encourage him to point out all the things he can see in them	96
frequently ask you the names of various objects and activities	good responses to his questions	try to be patient with the child and answer his questions, which will probably come thick and fast	97

As the baby grows, he will . . .	And so the baby needs . . .	You can help the baby learn if you . . .	Look at Activity #
point to the primary colors while you name them for him	to be told the colors of things, as you go about your daily business	help him to be aware that colors are different, and that they have different names	98

APPLE TREE ACADEMIES, INC.
PO BOX 4206
GREENSBORO, NC 27404

As the baby grows, he will . . .	And so the baby needs . . .	You can help the baby learn if you . . .	Look at Activity #
recognize you, his principal caregiver	frequent contact with you, his principal caregiver at the center, to reassure him that you'll be there for most of the day	try not to let totally unfamiliar people take him away where he can't see you	99
recognize other people that are important, but will probably be shy of strangers	opportunities to get to know and recognize others while he is with his principal caregiver	always reassure him and stay with him when strangers stop to chat or play with him	100
respond to his own image in a mirror	opportunities to recognize and get to know himself	let baby look at himself in the mirror and smile at and talk to himself; use his name and talk about what he sees	101
have emotional attachments to particular people, and begin to distinguish between their angry or friendly talking	many opportunities for interaction with familiar people	draw baby's attention to activities and other aspects of yourself and other familiar people; talk to him	102
begin to respond to more than one familiar person at a time	opportunities to play and interact in games and activities with more than one familiar person	let him try going back and forth from you to other people	103
respond well to his caregiver's actions, and begin to recognize his own name	activities that help him become aware of himself and that help his awareness of others	always use baby's name when you talk to him, and play with child to encourage him to respond to you	104
indicates his wants by gestures and vocalizations	good responses to his needs so that he feels that he is being successful at communicating	try to understand what baby is trying to say, and respond in an appropriate manner	105

SOCIAL/EMOTIONAL, 6—12 MONTHS

As the baby grows, he will . . .	And so the baby needs . . .	You can help the baby learn if you . . .	Look at Activity #
enjoy participating in games with others, and will perhaps offer toys to them if you prompt him	continued reassurance from you, so that he may now begin to tentatively accept and play with people he hasn't seen before	encourage him to play games with you and with others, but make sure that they are quiet, slow, simple, and non-threatening games	106

SOCIAL/EMOTIONAL, 12—18 MONTHS

be sociable, but self-contained and able to play alone for a short time	opportunities to be alone; to play by himself, but with you nearby, so that he knows where you are	give him toys and activities that encourage him to play alone	107
begin to imitate the actions and activities that you and others perform	opportunities to try to imitate actions that he sees going on around him	be available to show baby many activities that he can easily imitate, and encourage him to watch and imitate other people	108
show affectionate responses to you and others, or start other social contacts without your prompting	prompt return response from you, so that he enjoys his social person-to-person contacts	be sociable with him, and let him know that you are glad that he feels happy and affectionate and wants to show it	109
start to show the beginnings of various social emotions, such as affection, jealousy, sympathy, anxiety, etc.	to be able to demonstrate these emotions in a warm, supporting climate	respond to his various emotional moods, and help him to control them in a positive way	110
become more independent of you, and be able to better control his own actions and feelings	to "do" for himself, and to learn how to respond to his own feelings	let him try to do things on his own, and give him support when he does; let him move about the center on his own	111

As the baby grows, he will . . .	And so the baby needs . . .	You can help the baby learn if you . . .	Look at Activity #
try to achieve a sense of self-identity	to find out the difference between himself and others, and to find out who "he" is	encourage and applaud all of his attempts at performing for you, and his other ways of trying to find his "me"	112
follow simple commands and endure short waits to have his requests responded to	firm but affectionate handling to show him limits and guidelines for behavior	let him know what things he can do and what places he can go to, as patiently and as gently as you can	113
begin to be eager to get involved in the world around him, and want to try to do more and more	to be given the opportunity to try himself out	let him try many different things; take him on short walking trips; don't let him stay in one place too long	114
love to listen to music and to dance to it	songs and action rhymes with many body motions that he can perform	play music for him, sing songs for him, and let him try to sing them; use songs that will get child dancing and moving with the other children	115

SOCIAL/EMOTIONAL, 18—24 MONTHS

show affection for you and others that he knows	the people he knows and loves to respond to his showing of love	show baby much love and affection by responding to him when he shows you he loves you	116
do much watching and imitating of others	to play with others to build up knowledge of himself as separate from others	play games where baby can join with you and others	117

SOCIAL/EMOTIONAL, 18—24 MONTHS

As the baby grows, he will . . .	And so the baby needs . . .	You can help the baby learn if you . . .	Look at Activity #
begin to know what belongs to him and what belongs to others	his own place, such as a drawer, where he can keep his own favorite things	give baby a chance to achieve a new developmental step—the pride of ownership	118
recognize when people are happy, sad, angry, etc.	to learn that he can respond to these emotions	show baby how you feel about things, and encourage him to show his feelings and talk about them	119
be able to occupy himself and direct his own play, frequently pretending to be "mommy," etc.	time to play out activities that he has begun	encourage baby to play his own way and to increase his skills of imagination; let him know that you want him to "make believe" while he is playing	120
engage in "parallel play" with other children (children first play next to, but not with each other, in parallel play)	opportunities to play in this way without interruption from others	realize that this is an important developmental stage where baby learns about others	121

SOCIAL/EMOTIONAL, 24—30 MONTHS

sometimes tend to cling to the old, rather than to try the new	time to learn and think about each new experience	give him new experiences, with plenty of support and time for him to get used to them	122
respond to your requests sometimes, and sometimes do the opposite	a more mature type of handling, with your knowledge that this is another developmental phase	give him some reasons for doing things; try using toys and other things to attract him	123

As the baby grows, he will . . .	And so the baby needs . . .	You can help the baby learn if you . . .	Look at Activity #
use more imagination—his toys and dolls may represent other things to him	many articles that he must use his imagination with when he plays	enter into the spirit of his "make believe," and encourage him in it	124
have many contrary impulses, and not be able to make choices, changing his mind and moods quickly	opportunities to try both sides of various actions and activities, so he can learn about the results of various choices	try to be something of a "juggler" in handling his mood swings; it helps to have a sense of humor	125
enjoy being with other children, but may not be able to do so without getting into trouble	constant supervision when he is playing near or with others	realize that he sometimes has difficulty controlling his aggressive impulses, and needs to have you help him	126

As the baby grows, he will . . .	And so the baby needs . . .	You can help the baby learn if you . . .	Look at Activity #
look at and play with his fingers and toes	the opportunity to freely play and talk about the motions he makes	find ways to play with and talk to baby about his fingers, toes, and other body parts	127
babble and coo in "baby talk," instead of crying when he is alone	good language response from you and others	notice when the baby is babbling to himself, and make similar noises for him	128
turn his head when called by name, or when familiar objects are named	many opportunities to hear his own name and the names of objects	call baby by name as you talk to him; name the objects he sees	129
begin to repeat words or sounds of more than one syllable	practice in using this new language skill	imitate his sounds, and give him new words and sounds to try	130
begin to say real words, such as "Mama," "Dada," etc.	many opportunities to use new words, while relating them to the real person or object	respond enthusiastically whenever baby says a real word	131
begin to know what the names of many things are	to hear, often, the names of all the many objects he can see	tell baby the names of all the things you and he see and use all day	132

LANGUAGE, 12—18 MONTHS

As the baby grows, he will . . .	And so the baby needs . . .	You can help the baby learn if you . . .	Look at Activity #
begin to say several words, combined with his babbling, and try to use words to describe actions	opportunities to use his new words and to relate them to his or your actions	tell baby the names of the actions that you and he are doing	133
begin to know and name familiar objects and their owners	encouragement and help in naming things and their owners	reply to baby when he correctly names an object or owner by agreeing and repeating the name in a sentence	134
begin to name and point out familiar pictures in a book	colorful and large picture books and magazines to practice naming pictures	look at picture books and magazines with baby, letting him try to name familiar objects, or articles	135
take an interest in music and rhythm	opportunities to learn to do things with music	play and sing simple songs and do fingerplays with baby	136
begin to point to and name his body parts	many opportunities to learn and use the names of body parts	always refer to baby's hand, leg, etc. by name and encourage baby to repeat it	137
begin to understand when you ask him to do something	opportunities to hear and try to follow directions	show baby things he can do and say, by giving him simple directions	138

As the baby grows, he will . . .	And so the baby needs . . .	You can help the baby learn if you . . .	Look at Activity #
begin to understand how to use language	to use and practice all parts of speech (nouns, pronouns, verbs, etc.)	use many simple sentences as good examples for baby	139
begin to make phrases or short sentences of two or three words	to practice this new sentence-forming skill	encourage baby to try out his new skills; keep him talking	140
be able to recognize, name, and pick out common objects	to practice all of the time on his new naming and recognizing skills	let baby tell you what and where objects are	141
begin telling you about his needs, using sentences	to get a good response to his requests	always answer baby's requests; but don't always wait on him so that he has no need to ask	142
begin to use courtesy in speech, such as "please," "thank you"	courteous responses to his efforts at polite speech	always be polite to him—set a good example for him	143
continue asking many "what," "where," and "why" questions	correct answers to his questions, whenever possible	be patient with these questions; try to answer them honestly	144

LANGUAGE, 24—30 MONTHS

As the baby grows, he will . . .	And so the baby needs . . .	You can help the baby learn if you . . .	Look at Activity #
understand longer sentences, such as "When you finish lunch, Sonya, you can have a cookie."	to get used to hearing more complex, two-part sentences	speak to him in longer sentences; make sure he understands	145
talk more and more, since his speech is now coming in a rush	opportunities to talk without being "hushed" or "turned off"	let baby practice his talking with you and others; be very patient	146
sing or say nursery rhymes, songs and fingerplays	opportunities to take part in and enjoy these activities	give him and all the children a music session every day	147
begin to name and match colors, sizes, etc., and match words with what they do	opportunities to practice these new skills	see that baby has lots of time and the right kinds of toys to enlarge these skills	148
realize the difference between one and many; use plurals and proper tenses in speech	opportunities to practice these new skills	give baby many experiences and activities that will help him explore and learn these skills	149
use his imagination when playing	many items with which he can use his imagination	give baby many "props" that he can use for imaginative play	150

As the baby grows, he will . . .	And so the baby needs . . .	You can help the baby learn if you . . .	Look at Activity #
cry because he needs help	to be helped before he reaches hysteria	always be aware of what's happening	151
begin to hold his own bottle	to be allowed to do this when he wants to	just hand him his bottle, and let him take it from there	152
begin to try to feed himself	opportunities to learn to use his fingers and hands for eating	give baby finger foods to practice on, and give him time to practice	153
want to hold and try to use his drinking cup	help in learning how to handle a cup	help him learn, even if it is messy and takes a lot of time; be patient	154
reach for and try to use the spoon to feed himself	to learn how to use his spoon for eating	realize that baby is new at this, and so will spill more than he gets into his mouth	155
start trying to pick up things he has dropped	to practice a new skill: "picking up"	give him chances to "pick up" all kinds of objects	156
begin to take off clothing that he can remove easily	many times when it's alright to take things off	let child do as much as possible for himself when you undress him	157

SELF—CARE, 12—18 MONTHS

As the baby grows, he will . . .	And so the baby needs . . .	You can help the baby learn if you . . .	Look at Activity #
start to move freely about the center, on his own feet	to be allowed to walk around and practice "not holding on"	encourage him to walk on his own, if he can and wants to	158
ask you, by sounds and motions, for what he wants	response and help in learning to make himself understood	listen to child, and help him learn better ways to be understood	159
sometimes put out a foot or arm to help you while you dress him	to be told that you like it when he helps	show him the many ways he can help you as you dress him	160
show interest in trying to make his zippers work	to be shown how to handle a zipper	help him work with zippers; patience and time is required	161
begin to tell you that his diaper needs changing	prompt response to needs	matter-of-factly help him; he needs to feel good about his bodily functions	162
be able to sit still for a short while	to learn to sit on the potty chair occasionally	help him understand why he needs to become used to this new kind of seat	163

As the baby grows, he will . . .	And so the baby needs . . .	You can help the baby learn if you . . .	Look at Activity #
start to help when you wash his hands	to learn how, when, and why he should wash his hands	encourage him to do as much as he can while his hands are washed	164
be able to eat and drink with only a little spilling	to be allowed to use the spoon and cup for himself at meals	realize that this is necessary for baby to learn, even if it is time-consuming and perhaps messy	165
be able to dress himself in a simple garment	chances to try to dress himself	let him try, even though you could probably dress him quicker	166
begin to help you pick up toys	to be encouraged to help you	help him understand why we have to pick up toys and other things	167
know and tell you when he needs the toilet	immediate response to his signals	help him to realize, in a gentle way, that the toilet is the place for body wastes	168

SELF—CARE, 24—30 MONTHS

As the baby grows, he will . . .	And so the baby needs . . .	You can help the baby learn if you . . .	Look at Activity #
be able to remove much of his clothing by himself, and be able to put some things on	freedom and time to try to dress and undress himself	give baby a chance to learn to be independent	169

SELF—CARE, 24—30 MONTHS

As the baby grows, he will . . .	And so the baby needs . . .	You can help the baby learn if you . . .	Look at Activity #
be able to eat and drink quite well, with hardly any spilling	to feed himself even though he'll probably take a long time	give him his food and let him do the rest for himself	170
put toys away when he's asked	storage areas that are easy for him to reach and use	let child put his own things away, even though he'll take longer than you would	171
use the spigot and get his own glass of water	to be allowed to wait on himself	give him any assistance he needs, but let him do what he can for himself	172
rarely have "accidents," since he is totally toilet-trained	praise for success, and non-critical help when he does have an "accident"	avoid making baby feel bad or guilty about "accidents"	173

Hang a mobile over the child's crib, or even better, hang one on each side of the crib. Be sure that the baby cannot reach them and pull them down on himself. As the bright objects sway and turn, the baby will try to use his eyes to follow them. He'll spend more time looking if the objects vary in brightness and darkness, and if they move frequently.

Make a shadow box and hang it near the crib where it can be seen by the baby. Here's how:

HOW TO MAKE A SHADOW BOX:

Materials:
- *shoe box
- *construction paper
- *glue
- *scissors
- *thread
- *artificial flowers and leaves
- *aluminum foil
- *cardboard
- *tape

Procedure:
1. Line box with colored paper.
2. Glue or tape artificial leaves and flowers on outside of box.
3. Cut out the shape of a large airplane from cardboard.
4. Cover airplane with foil.
5. Tie threads to airplane and hang it in the box.
6. Use your imagination—find other colorful objects to replace the airplane. Give the baby a change of pace.

Play with a rattle while the baby watches. Stand behind him so that he can see the rattle but not you. Hold it a little above his face and gently shake it. When he looks up at it, move it in a slow circle so that he can watch it by just moving his eyes, not by moving his head. After a while, move the rattle in the other direction.

After the baby learns to do this, move the rattle in a curve from above his head to right above his shoulders. This will make the baby turn his head to watch. Now he's using both his eyes and his head. Try it on the other side.

Help the baby practice grasping. Hand him an object—a favorite toy, for instance—from one side and then from the other. Hold it close to him, and then let him reach for it. If he grabs it, let him play with it for a short time. Be careful not to frustrate him. Don't forget to vary the objects, so he can learn that different things feel different. A good toy to help the baby learn to change the ways he grasps is a bean bag.

HOW TO MAKE A RATTLE OR SHAKER:

Materials:
*small plastic pill bottles
or
aluminum juice cans
*permanent weatherproof glue

*colorful plastic tape
*non-toxic paint
*bells, beads, beans, pebbles
*contact paper

Procedure:
1. Put objects such as bells, beads, etc. into your collection of pill bottles or juice cans.
2. Glue lids on bottles with strong glue. (Regular white glue is not strong enough.)
3. When glue has dried, tape around lids several times with plastic tape.
4. Paint faces and designs on bottles.
5. Cover juice cans with several thicknesses of plastic tape or contact paper.

HOW TO MAKE SPOOL DOLLS:

Materials:
*15-20 empty thread spools of various sizes
* ¼ " wide elastic cording
*non-toxic paint

Procedure:
1. Paint spools, let dry.
2. Use large spool for head and 10-12 small spools for body, arms, legs.
3. Tie two cross pieces of elastic (arms and legs) onto a larger center piece (body).
4. Thread spools on elastic, knotting it between each spool.
5. Tie double knots after end spools.
6. Paint face on spool for head.

Make wrist bands for the baby. Sometimes you can put one on the baby's right wrist, and sometimes on his left. These will help the baby to learn to move his hands where he wants them so that he can see the wrist bands. You can put the bands on the baby's ankles sometimes, to give him experience in moving his feet, too.

HOW TO MAKE WRIST BANDS:

Materials: *children's socks (with striped tops, if you can get them)
*needle and thread
*red felt scraps
*black felt marker (non-toxic)
*scissors

Procedure: 1. Cut the top off of each sock.
2. Cut small circles from felt for the faces.
3. Make smiling faces on felt with black felt marker.
4. Sew at least four faces around the band (sock top).

If you put a small, brightly colored sock mitten over each hand, the baby can practice finding his hands with these, also.

HOW TO MAKE SOCK MITTENS:

Materials: *two bright colored infant socks
*scissors
*needle and thread

Procedure: 1. Cut a small slit for the baby's thumb in the heel of the socks.
2. Cut off the toe portion of the socks for the baby's fingers.
3. Hem the cut edges.

4

Give the baby his own spoon at feeding time, and be patient with him when he tries to use it himself.

Make a finger glove for you and the baby to play with. When you use it, hold your hand directly in front of the baby's body.

HOW TO MAKE A FINGER GLOVE:

Materials: *old glove
*different fabrics (for example, felt, fur, silk, burlap, corduroy)
*needle and thread

Procedure: 1. Sew different fabric pieces on each finger of the glove.
2. Place glove on your hand.
3. Let the baby grasp each of your fingers in turn.

5

Show the baby a favorite toy or other interesting object, and then move it off to the side. Try to get the baby to turn sideways and reach for it.

Put a toy at his side, and let him turn sideways and reach for it. Then put it on the other side. Always let him play with it for a while when he grabs it. Remember not to frustrate him.

6

Hand the baby a toy by first giving it to one hand, and then to the other. Pretty soon the baby will begin to transfer the toy from one hand to the other all by himself. If he doesn't, show him how by doing it yourself.

7

Hang a busy box on the baby's crib. Then he can practice on it whenever he wants to. This toy gives the baby a chance to practice his skills of getting hold of something and making it move the way he wants. If the objects on the busy box make noises and spin around when the baby hits them, it will be even better. Make sure the baby can reach it with both his hands and his feet. Be sure to change objects occasionally to keep the baby interested. *(See Activity #61 for directions.)*

8

When the baby is being fed, put a small piece of cracker or cereal in front of him. You'll see that at first the baby will be able to touch it, but not be able to pick it up. Help him learn by putting his forefinger and thumb on it. Put your fingers on top of his. He will slowly but surely learn how to pick it up by himself. At first he'll scoop it up with his whole hand, but after a while, he'll be using only his thumb and forefinger, as you demonstrated. Now he has learned the pincher grip.

A good toy to help the baby practice his pincher grip is a ring and spindle toy. This is a toy where a straight, upright wooden spindle is attached to a base. Wooden rings fit down over the spindle, one on top of the other. Start the baby with just one ring, and as he learns to place this on the spindle, give him more rings. Don't worry if he doesn't get them in the right order.

Play a hide-and-seek game with the baby. To play this, use a box and a blanket, and hide a toy under one of them. Let the baby try to find the toy.

When the baby can find the toy the first time, make the game a little harder. This time wrap the toy in the blanket, and then put the blanket inside the box. Show him how to find it, and then let him try to find it on his own. The idea is that the baby has to open two things to find the toy. Two boxes with loose lids can be used, too—place the toy in one box, put the lid on, then put it in the second box and put it's lid on. This will be a real challenge for the baby. Make sure he sees you hide it, and stop if he can't find it and gets too frustrated.

Get a plastic see-through shoe box, and put some toys in it. Let the baby try to take off the lid and get the toys all by himself.

Hide a toy behind a tray that you are holding upright in front of the baby. If he can't find the toy, let a part of the toy stick out from behind the tray.

Use a toy or an object that has a handle on top, such as a bell. Give it to the baby upside down, so he has to turn it over to make it work.

Turn several toys upside down and put them in a line in front of the baby. See if the baby can turn them right side up again.

Cut out the bottom of a cereal box to make a tunnel. Tell the baby that you are pushing a toy truck through the tunnel, and ask him to watch for it to come out the other end.

Fold a piece of cardboard in half to make a hill. Put a toy truck at the top, and let it slide down. The baby will be fascinated and want to try it.

Tin or plastic measuring cups that fit inside each other are good things for the baby to play with to see how things fit and to compare size. You can also let the baby experiment with pots and pans that fit inside each other; boxes and tin cans can also be used. Make sure all sharp edges are covered to protect the baby from harm.

10

After the baby can transfer things from one hand to another fairly easily, try handing him a third toy when he already has a toy in each hand. He will probably try to grab the third toy while his hands are full. But with practice, he will soon learn to put one toy down first. Let him figure this one out for himself.

See if the baby will give you one of his toys as he reaches for a third one. He needs to learn that he can give up a toy or object for a while, and that it will still be available when he wants it again.

11

Line large plastic containers with materials of various textures, such as fake fur, corduroy, or felt. Then put interesting toys inside them. The baby will reach for the toys, and at the same time will feel the lining materials.

Something else the baby will enjoy is a bean bag face puppet.

HOW TO MAKE A BEAN BAG FACE PUPPET:

Materials:
*felt, or other heavy serviceable fabric
*beans
*needle and thread
*scissors

Procedure:
1. Cut from the felt two circles approximately 5″ in diameter.
2. Cut face features (eyes, nose, mouth, etc.) from felt; make one face a happy one, the other sad.
3. Sew the faces on the felt circles.
4. Sew the felt circles together, face side out, leaving a small opening to insert the beans.
5. Put the beans inside, stuffing the bean bag to the amount of plumpness you want.
6. Sew up the opening.

Another thing the baby will enjoy is a tote bag. He can wear it over his shoulders, and carry his toys around in it. Let him try to find certain toys in it for you. He might also enjoy playing "mail carrier."

HOW TO MAKE A TOTE BAG:

Materials: *2 pieces of felt, canvas or denim, approximately 12″ by 20″ in size
*felt scraps of various colors

Procedure: 1. Cut two strips 12″ long and 2″ wide off the end of each piece of fabric to use for handles; hem raw edges.
2. Sew the large pieces of fabric together on three sides, making a bag roughly 11″ wide and 17½″ deep.
3. Hem top edge of bag.
4. Sew the handles firmly to each side of the bag.
5. Decorate the bag with colored felt scraps in your own designs.

Find a cardboard tube (the center from a roll of paper towels will do). Then get a small toy car that will fit through the tube, and roll the car through it. See if the baby will watch for the car to come out the other end.

Here are some other interesting things to make that will involve the baby in different kinds of action.

HOW TO MAKE A MATCH BOX PICTURE TOY:

Materials: *match box (the large box for kitchen matches is best)
*small, colorful pictures from a book or magazine
*glue (non-toxic)

Procedure: 1. Glue pictures both on the inside and the outside of the box.
2. Show the baby how he can push the drawer of the match box in and out to see the pictures.

HOW TO MAKE A "PAT" PICTURE BOOK:

Materials: *needle and thread
*several pieces of felt, at least 6″ x 6″
*materials such as cotton balls, pieces of sponge, sandpaper, etc. and scraps of various kinds of fabric (velvet, fake fur, etc.)

Procedure: 1. Sew the pieces of felt together on one side to form a book.
2. On each page, draw, paste, or sew a colorful picture.
3. Paste or sew on each picture, an appropriate scrap of the materials you have gathered. For example, a cotton ball makes a perfect rabbit tail. Here's a chance to use some of your creativity.
4. Name and talk about each picture with the baby as he touches and pats the pictures.

13

If you have a small sliding board available, try rolling a ball down it as the baby watches. Then let him try it.

Line up two or three chairs. Then roll the ball under them, and let the baby retrieve it for you. Let the baby try his hand at rolling the ball under the chairs.

Ask the baby to stand up for you. Make sure he has something firm to hold on to. Then take a doll or other favorite toy and stand it up where the baby can reach it, while still standing and holding on with one hand. Encourage the baby to grab the toy and throw it away. Then place the toy in another place he can reach, and let him try again. Keep the baby moving from place to place to reach the toy.

Play a game of ball-rolling with the baby. Roll it to him, and let him try to roll it back. Here's a little song you can sing while you and the baby play with the ball:

> We roll the ball, it's rolling,
> Now roll it down the track.
> I will roll it down to him (her),
> And *(baby's name)* will roll it back.

14

Find a large box (a shoe box is good) and cut a good-sized hole in the lid. Show the baby how to drop large wooden beads or blocks through the hole into the box. Then show him how to reach in through the hole, and get the objects out again. He'll keep busy for quite some time putting them in and taking them out.

Put some small crackers or cereal bits in a plastic screw top container. Then screw the lid on very loosely. Show the baby how to take off the lid and get the goodies.

Get a finished wooden puzzle, and let the baby take the pieces out of the frame. Show him how to get started.

Give the baby some clothespins. Show him how to place them around the edge of a box (a coffee can may be used if it hasn't got any sharp edges).

A doodad tray is fun for the baby and if you supervise it well, it will be fun for you too.

HOW TO MAKE A DOODAD TRAY:

Materials: *muffin tin
*small toys and doodads (such as measuring spoons, empty spools, jar lids, etc.)

Procedure: 1. Fill several cups of the muffin tin with small toys and doodads.
2. Show the baby how to take these objects out of one of the cups and drop them into the next one.

15

Put a spoon and a cup in front of the baby. Show him how to put the spoon into the cup. The child may try to do this himself without waiting for you to demonstrate how to do it. He may miss the cup, because putting something into a small space takes practice. If he's had plenty of practice on the activities in *#14*, he will probably be good at this one in a short time.

As you feed the baby, let him have an empty spoon to play with. Of course, he will want to put his spoon into the food, too. Take advantage of this enthusiasm, and help him to fill his spoon and try to put it into his mouth. He'll lose a lot on the way, but practice will improve his style.

Turn the baby loose with a large tub of cornmeal, rice, or salt. Give him some spoons and containers of various sizes. He'll have a glorious time and make a huge mess, but he'll also be learning to handle tableware. Supervise this activity, especially if more than one child is involved, and you can be sure that all will go smoothly.

16

Now the baby is ready for the big step of drinking from a cup. You should always use an unbreakable cup as you help him learn this new skill. Make sure the cup is of a size and shape that the baby can hold with both hands. At first, you might give him an empty cup to practice holding on to while he drinks from another one you are holding for him. He'll soon let you know that he wants to hold the cup himself while he drinks. Put just a few drops of something you know he likes, such as juice, into the cup and let him try to drink it himself. At first there is sure to be a lot of spilling, so a little at a time works out much better. As the baby improves this skill, you can gradually increase the amount you put in the cup for him.

17

If the baby has been doing well on previous activities and can handle small objects quite well with his fingers, he can now try blocks. They are excellent playthings because so many things can be done with them. At first only a few blocks should be used, so the baby won't be overwhelmed by them.

Play with the baby and his blocks. Seat him and yourself comfortably on the floor with a few blocks. Show him how one block can be put on top of another. He may be anxious to try this himself. Then try placing another block on top, making a tower of three. Let the baby try this. Don't worry if the baby doesn't make each block line up exactly with the one beneath. One important feature of this activity is that it is self-correcting. If the baby doesn't put the blocks on right, they all will come tumbling down. The baby will have as much fun watching them fall as he does building them up.

A simple and inexpensive block set of a good size can be made easily.

HOW TO MAKE A BLOCK SET:

Materials: *several small milk cartons (quart size)
*contact paper in a pretty color or print

Procedure: 1. Cut milk cartons so they are in about a 3″ or 4″ cube shape.
2. Fasten an extra piece of cardboard to the open side of the cube.
3. Cover cube with contact paper.

After the baby has had success with blocks that are all the same size, he can use blocks of larger and smaller sizes. If blocks of different sizes are used at first, they will only confuse the baby, and cut down on the number of times he can successfully build a tower.

Let the baby play with soft blocks, made of sponge rubber or soft plastic, also. These blocks have a different "feel," and provide varied experiences for him.

18

The larger the piece of paper the baby has to practice drawing on, the better it will be for his developing motor coordination. Grocery bags cut to lay flat, or large pieces of cardboard cut from boxes or cartons can be used, as well as the largest size of blank newsprint. He should also have large crayons, easy for his small hand to grasp. Remember, the process of using the crayons is much more important than the result for the baby. So don't show or tell him what to draw or how you think it should look. Let him choose his own colors and do it his own way.

Make space to hang all the children's pictures up. You can print their names on them, and tell them that this is how their name looks. A low clothesline gives a lot of space for hanging up pictures. Make sure it is low enough so that the children can stand in front of their pictures and see them easily. The line should be arranged so that the tallest child can walk under it. This will prevent accidents.

19

Try to use picture books that have bright colors and uncomplicated pictures that the baby can easily see and understand. The best books for babies have only one idea or picture on each page. Make sure they are large enough for the baby's small hands to work with easily. They should only have one or two printed words. Remember, the baby can only "read" the pictures. Books made from heavy paper, cardboard, or even cloth will last much longer.

Be sure to sit down with the baby every so often, and "read" with him. Sit in a comfortable chair, with the baby in your lap, and look at the book with him. He'll probably get interested in the page turning operation, and want to try it himself. Don't worry if he skips pages. As you look at each new page, talk to the baby about the picture and what it means. Let him "talk" about them too. You can give the baby a pleasant reading experience when you hold him comfortably, and take time to talk over the picture as you and he look at the book. You are helping the baby develop motor control by letting him hold the book and turn the pages. You are also getting the baby started on the first step toward learning to read.

Give the baby some old magazines or catalogs from mail order houses. He will enjoy looking at these, both alone and with you.

20

Most toddlers like to pull things out of drawers, cabinets, baskets, etc. So you can keep the baby happy for a long time if you give him a big box full of old Christmas cards and other greeting cards, colorful pieces of junk mail, etc. He'll pull them out and inspect them. Try to have some envelopes with papers inside that he can pull out.

Another box or drawer filled with old pots and pans, pie plates, lids, empty cans, spoons (metal and wooden), plastic cups, etc., will fascinate him for a long while.

If you have an old metal coffee pot, give this to the baby and let him take it apart. (Don't give him any glass parts.)

Put a puppet on the baby's hand and let him manipulate it. Here's how to make a simple one out of a mitten.

HOW TO MAKE A MITTEN PUPPET:

Materials: *child's mitten   *yarn
                 *buttons   *needle and thread

Procedure: 1. Sew buttons on mitten for eyes.
                 2. Embroider a nose and mouth on the mitten with yarn.

As mentioned in *Activity #15*, a large tub of cornmeal, rice, or salt provides an excellent opportunity for the baby to learn to use his hands. In addition to the items indicated in *Activity #15*, give him funnels, sieves, and other interesting kitchen items to use.

21

If the baby has been doing well with all of these activities so far, he can try a jar with a screw-on lid. Make sure the jar is large and unbreakable; plastic is best. Show the baby how to work the lid, and then put it back on, loosely. Let him try. Put something in the jar, put the lid on, then let the baby try to get the lid off and the object out of the jar. You'll find that he will enjoy this new game. He'll spend a lot of time putting things in the jar and putting the lid on, and then reversing the process. If however, you find that the baby is becoming frustrated, stop and try again at a later time.

This type of activity not only helps the baby develop motor control of his hands, but also helps introduce him to the orderly concepts of "off and on," and "in and out."

22

Encourage the baby to do a lot of spontaneous scribbling. He needs to do lots and lots of scribbling before he can control his hand to make it do what he wants it to do.

Another thing that will help develop the baby's eye-hand coordination is water "painting." Give the child a brush (at least 2" wide) and a small bucket of water and let him "paint" anything he chooses. Let him try it indoors as well as outside in the yard or on the porch, on objects that water won't damage.

23

APPLE TREE ACADEMIES, INC.
PO BOX 4206
GREENSBORO, NC 27404

Give the baby a string of large pop beads and let him discover how to pull them apart. Demonstrate the first one. Give him several large containers to put the beads in, and then he can play with them by moving them from container to container.

Putting the beads together again will be much harder. You can show him how, but he probably won't be able to do it until he is older.

When you start the baby with these beads, make sure he understands they are *not* to be put in his mouth. If you feel that there is any danger of his swallowing the beads, don't use them.

Squeeze toys are good for strengthening fingers. The activities listed in *#14* are also good.

24

Eating small tidbits is good for giving the baby practice in eye-hand manipulation. Put small foods such as raisins, cereal bits, or cheese cubes within the baby's reach, and he'll get lots of practice as he tries to pick them up and eat them.

Try giving the baby a plastic container to put these foods in and out of (that is, if he doesn't eat them all first).

If you have a plastic bottle, give it to the baby with some clothespins. Show him how to put the clothespins in the bottle, and then shake them out again. He may need your help with this game at first.

Take a shoe-box, and make two or three holes of various sizes and shapes in the lid. Then show the baby how to push or drop different objects through the holes. He'll find out that some things fit in one hole and not another. After he gets everything in the box, show him that he can take the lid off and start over. Let him play this new game for as long as he seems to be interested. Just be sure that none of the items used are small enough to swallow, unless you can stay with him as he plays with these things.

25

While they are learning, babies will rip and tear things apart. Give the baby a stack of old magazines and newspapers that he can use for anything he chooses.

Show him how to tear without grabbing, and how to poke holes in the paper with the handle of a wooden spoon. He'll have a wonderful time and make a paper snowstorm around himself.

Tearing and poking give the baby exercise for his small hand muscles. This is also a good way for the baby to get rid of any aggressive feelings.

A hole puncher will fascinate the baby. Show him how it works and let him punch holes in newspaper.

26

Since the baby can only follow one simple direction at a time, you'll have to use constant talk. As the baby follows each direction, give him the next one. For example, say "Ella, bring your shoes to me." When the baby does that, then say "Hold your foot out, Ella, while we put your shoe on." It's a good idea to constantly describe the actions as you give the baby directions. For example, say "Hold your hands up so we can put your sweater on, Marva."

Help the baby as much as he needs to be helped, but remember that it's more important for the baby to learn to do things for himself than for you to save a few minutes by doing them for him.

Another thing the baby needs to learn is to wash and dry his hands. Do it first yourself, then let the baby try. Many demonstrations and much practice will probably have to follow until the baby can perform these operations on his own.

Wrapping small toys in foil or tissue paper will help the baby develop small muscles at the same time that he's having fun unwrapping them. Remember not to use string or ribbon, since these may be harmful to the baby.

If you have an old jacket with buttons or a zipper, and dresses or other old clothes with large snaps or hooks, give them to the baby to play "dress-up" with. This way he can also get a chance to practice using zippers, snaps, etc. You can even sew large buttons, snaps, etc. on an old blouse or dress so the baby can use them. Remember that such things must be large and easy for the baby's small fingers to handle.

27

Now may be a good time to start the baby working with simple puzzles. Show him one while it's together, and talk about the picture, point out the parts, etc. Then let the baby dump the pieces out. Show him how the pieces have color only on one side, while the other side is rough and dull. Show him how one piece fits together with another. Let him try fitting the pieces together, helping him when he gets stuck. Show him how to turn a piece around and around to find where it fits. The baby's first puzzles should be very simple with no more than three pieces.

Try using blocks of different shapes, such as squares, rectangles, and triangles. Let the baby play with them whatever way he wants. Don't worry about the names of these shapes yet. The baby is still too young to learn these concepts. He will be happy just pushing, piling, or banging the blocks. He will, however, have been exposed to the concept of things having different shapes.

Experiment with flat shapes also. Cut out a square from a piece of cardboard, leaving a frame around three sides of the piece you cut out. Leave the fourth side open. Show the baby how to slide the square back into the frame, and make it fit nicely. Let him try to do it. He'll enjoy sliding it in and out, as soon as he learns how.

Now make a harder puzzle. Cut a square from the center of a piece of cardboard, leaving a frame on four sides. The baby will discover that he has to jiggle and slide this piece around to make it fit. You'll be helping him learn about shapes and sizes, edges and location.

If you want to make these flat shape puzzles more sturdy so they'll last longer, cover them with pretty and colorful contact paper.

If the baby has really been interested in these flat shape puzzles, you can also make them with circles or triangles.

Only give the baby one flat puzzle shape at a time at first. When he becomes proficient at these, you can give him two different shapes, but only one frame. Let him figure out which one it goes in all by himself, with no help from you.

The baby will soon be able to graduate into form board activities. You can buy a form board, but if you want to make one, just cut three various shapes (circle, square, triangle) out of one piece of wood. Put knobs on the cut out shapes, and sand and paint them. Let the baby try to fit the right shapes into the right forms. He may be confused by all of the shapes, at first. Show him how to use the form board, but stop if the baby seems frustrated or not interested. There will always be another time. If the child wants to, you can let him play with and explore the shapes and board on his own. He may learn more that way.

28

You can make your own play-dough if you have no clay:

HOW TO MAKE PLAY-DOUGH:

Materials: *1 cup salt   *2 tbs. salad oil
                *1½ cups flour   *few drops of food coloring
                *½ cup water

Procedure: 1. Add food coloring to water.
                2. Mix salt, flour, water and salad oil together until you get a good consistency for modeling.

When you make play-dough, let the children participate by choosing the color they want. They'll also enjoy helping "knead" the dough to the proper consistency.

When the children are finished playing with it, wrap it in plastic and store it in the refrigerator until next time.

The children can also make models with it. The models can be left out to harden.

Don't worry if the children put this dough in their mouths. It doesn't taste good, but it won't hurt them.

When the children are playing with play-dough, let them sit at a table or on the floor. Use a cookie sheet, or tape down some plastic for a work space. If you dust their hands with a little flour, the dough won't stick to their fingers as much. Give them cookie cutters, rolling pins, forks, spoons, etc. to enjoy working with in the play-dough.

Another good finger and hand activity is fingerpainting. Children need these outlets of messy playing and clay pounding. It helps them get rid of feelings of anxiety or hostility.

You can give each child a sheet of coated paper for fingerpainting, but you might find that for first timers at this activity, an old tray or cookie sheet works better.

Old shirts that open down the back or aprons are a "must" for these kinds of play. Perhaps you'll find it's a good idea to use old newspapers to cover the area where the children are working.

Here's an easy recipe for fingerpaint.

HOW TO MAKE FINGERPAINT:

Materials:
*flour
*salt
*water
*food coloring

Procedure:
1. Mix flour and a little salt with water until you get a thick, gravy-like base.
2. Divide into various portions and color each with food colors.
3. Let the children help decide on the colors to use.

29

Bead stringing is a good activity to help children learn to use their hands. It develops eye-hand coordination. Make sure the beads are too big to be swallowed. Let the child play with the beads and string for a while, and see if he discovers how to string them. You may have to help him. Let him hold the string while you put a bead on, and then let him try while you hold the string. When the beads are strung, he will love to wear them as a necklace. Just tie the two ends of the string together. You might find the child is not interested, or is getting frustrated. If this happens, he is probably not ready to learn this skill. In that case, just let him play with the beads if he wants to, or let him do something else.

It's very important, at this stage of the baby's development, for him to have a large selection of manipulative toys and materials. Some things you should provide for him are large snap beads, large stringing beads, toy cars and trucks, dolls, puzzles, and sorting boxes. Natural materials, such as sand, rice, water, or even whipped cream are all very good manipulative toys, since the children have to use their hands to play with them.

30

Remember that children of this age won't sit still for very long. Read to the baby only for as long as he seems really interested. If he starts turning pages fast and in big clumps, you'll know he's starting to get tired. Stop reading to him, and let him have the book to play with alone for as long as he wants to. He may sit and look at the pictures as he turns page after page himself.

The baby may also turn the book upside down, or start to tear it up. This, too, is normal behavior for children at this stage of development. If he starts to become destructive, you can show him that you value the book by quietly removing it and replacing it with a sturdier toy. By setting a good example yourself of how books should be treated, you are helping the baby to learn.

31

Let the baby help you fold paper. To teach him how to fold, you can say "Let's see if you can fold the paper, Rodney. Watch, and then you can try. First, I bend the paper and then press it down flat. Now I'll fold it for you, and you can press it down." You might have to guide the baby's hand with yours at first. Keep letting him try until the paper has been folded several times.

With this kind of activity, the baby will learn that new shapes can be made from old shapes. Other folding materials that the baby will enjoy working with are pipe cleaners and aluminum foil.

32

The baby needs to experiment with size and shape. Give him lots of things to use for this. The baby can try putting round things into square things, or the other way around. Let him put small things into bigger things. Show the child how to feel the edges of various shapes so that he can tell a round shape without even opening his eyes. Use your imagination and look around to find many things that the baby can use for these experiments.

Another way to help the baby learn to trace shapes with his fingers is to give him cut-out shapes in sandpaper or other textured materials.

Remember that peg boards, form boards and large simple puzzles are also good for teaching differences in shapes and sizes.

Try to find a set of five boxes that nest inside each other. You can save old cardboard boxes of the right sizes, and cover them with contact paper to make them last longer. Wooden nesting boxes can be made or purchased.

A set of nesting boxes can also be turned over and stacked up like a tower.

Play some games with the baby using these boxes. Show him that when you place a smaller box inside a bigger one, it almost disappears from sight. Or, even more interesting, turn one box upside down over a smaller one, so that the child has to look for the little box. "Look, Iris, all gone—Where did it go?" The baby will show you. Then see if the baby can do it. If the child loses interest in your games, let him play with the boxes by himself.

Nesting cans that you can make yourself are good for this kind of play also.

HOW TO MAKE NESTING CANS:

Materials: *empty cans that nest inside of each other
            *contact paper or paint (non-toxic)

Procedure: 1. Collect cans until you have four or five sizes that will fit neatly into each other.
            2. Be sure that there are no sharp rims or edges that might cut fingers.
            3. Cover the cans with contact paper, or paint them in attractive colors.

33

The baby should have crayons and paper that he can scribble on. Let him do as he pleases. Don't give him a model to copy, or tell him to draw only a certain thing. Just let him "free wheel." His work doesn't have to please grown-ups. It's enough that it pleases him.

On occasion, however, you might sit down and play a game with him. Let him make a mark, then you can draw a line just like it. The baby will probably enjoy this (he loves to have your attention for himself), but if he doesn't, don't force him. Just let him draw his own thing.

34

The baby is now able to enjoy more complex toys. You'll notice that almost anything that the baby finds becomes a manipulative toy. The baby is getting more control of his hands and feet, and so he starts exploring, investigating and examining everything he can see, touch or grab. Keep a collection of kitchen utensils (egg beaters, big spoons, pots and pans, funnels, etc.) for the baby to use whenever he wants to.

You'll also notice that the baby is trying to use his manipulative skills to help you as you dress him, or do other routines with him. He'll grab his zippers, buttons, or snaps in an effort to make them work. He'll want to turn the faucet off or on, pull off a paper towel, flush the toilet. These are all good things for the baby to try. The child needs much practice in using and handling things with his hands.

Put a door-hook or a latch on an old wooden cigar box. Show the baby how it works, and then let him try. He'll play alone with this new toy for a long time.

35

Some good problem-solving toys are nesting boxes, a lock box (like the cigar box described in *#34*), rack-a-stack, sorting boxes, or puzzles. Most of these toys are self-correcting—they only work one way, so the baby knows when he is right or wrong. It's important for him to have immediate feedback on whether he has gotten something right, especially when he's playing alone. Notice also that much hand and finger action is needed to play with these toys. This is good for eye-hand coordination. These toys also develop the baby's problem-solving abilities, so important for later success in school. You'll also find that these kinds of toys are played with over and over again because they are challenging, stimulating, and fun to play with.

36

Help the baby with arm exercises. Move his arms up over his head and down again. Do one arm at a time, then both together, and then go back to one at a time. Varying the motions will keep the baby interested. Next time, put his arms out to the side, together and separately, as you did when putting them over his head.

Here's a sing-song jingle you can say as you do these exercises with the baby:

> Little bird, little bird, fly about,
> First fly in, and then fly out,
> Start down low, and then go up high,
> Little bird, little bird, learn to fly.

For leg exercises, turn the baby on his back. Now push his legs up into a knee-bend position. Do them one at a time, and then together, as you did with his arms. Here's a jingle for leg exercises:

> Chug-chug-chug-chug, down the street,
> Up and down go baby's feet,
> Chug-chug-chug-chug, one, two, three,
> I love you and you love me."

All of these exercises will help the baby develop a sense of his own body image.

37

Rattle a rattle where the baby can hear it. He'll become interested, and will have to twist and turn his whole body to find it. See if you can make him turn over, or try to sit up. Be careful not to frustrate the baby, though. When he has found the rattle, he'll probably reach for it. Give it to him so he can play with it. If you do this several times a week with the baby, he'll be getting lots of good body exercise.

Another fun game that will give the baby lots of exercise is to blow up a balloon and bat it around with him. Try not to scare him by letting him grab it and break it.

38

The baby should always be dressed in the minimum amount of loose clothing, so his movements will be unrestricted. He needs to be able to move and turn about easily.

Help the baby exercise to strengthen his back and learn to sit up. When the baby is on his back, pull him up in a sitting position, and let him down again. Do this several times, or for as long as the baby enjoys it. Soon he may be able to pull himself up while holding onto your hands. Here's a chant you can use as he exercises in this up-and-down "see-saw" fashion.

> Up my little bundle comes,
> Down my little bundle goes.
> Peek around, have you found,
> Baby's wiggly toes?

This game will help the baby to strengthen his back and stomach muscles, as well as his arms and legs. He'll like it because he can see the world from a different angle each time he sits up.

39

A nice shiny pan that the baby can see himself in will encourage arm motions. The baby will reach for his reflection and pat it, or bang it. The baby himself will invent things to do with the pan.

Get two aluminum pie plates, and show the baby how he can bang them together. Then let him try it.

Attach a short ribbon to the head of a soft rag doll. Show the baby how he can hold the ribbon and make the doll dance.

Another toy that the baby will find interesting to shake and play with is a "Jingle-Jangle Fish." It has a nice tail that jingles.

HOW TO MAKE A "JINGLE-JANGLE FISH":

Materials: *large empty plastic bottle *colored plastic tape
*short shoe lace *felt pen (non-toxic)
*juice can lids

Procedure:
1. Tape the edges of the juice can lids with plastic tape to cover all of the rough or sharp edges.
2. Punch a hole in the center of each lid.
3. Paint eyes, scales, and fins on the bottle with the felt pen, making it look like a fish.
4. Make a hole in the bottom of the bottle.
5. Thread shoe lace through the hole in the bottle; attach it firmly with a double knot inside the bottle.
6. String the lids on the shoe lace (this is the fish's tail).
7. Put a large bead or pebble inside the bottle to make it rattle.
8. Replace cap on bottle, and tape it firmly in place.

40

As you bounce the baby on your knee, let him see and hear you clap the rhythm. You can also hold his hands and let him help you clap.

Use a drum or tambourine to keep the rhythm. Play different rhythms on it, and perhaps the baby will begin to recognize distinct changes in them.

Maybe the baby would like a rhythm instrument of his own. Give him an old round cereal box to use as a drum. A wooden spoon will make a fine drum stick.

Be sure to let the baby spend some time in a bounce chair or baby swing. He'll love the motion he feels, especially since he can make it himself.

The baby will probably also enjoy the motion of a larger outdoor swing, if you sit on it and hold him in your lap. Rock him while you sing "Rock-a-bye, Baby."

Hold the baby in your arms as you dance to music.

Hold the baby by the hands, and show him how to do deep-knee bends. This can also be done to music. After the baby learns this game, you might have a hard time getting him to stop.

41

Find an object that has some stretch or "give" to it. An old sock will do, or you can make a simple toy from a spool and a piece of fairly wide elastic. Dangle this object in front of the baby, but out of reach, so that he has to stretch to get it. Use words that describe what is happening as you play with him. Say things like "Come on, Aaron, grab for it," or "Let's see if you can catch it this time, Jewel." When the baby has a good grasp on the object, pull on it so there's no stretch between your hand and his. Try to get him to pull back on his end. Maybe you can get a pulling game started where you pull, and then release, so that the baby can pull. Let him use both hands if he wants to. Don't let the article "snap" back at him, though. You wouldn't want to scare or tease him. Keep playing as long as the baby seems interested.

Give the baby many and various objects to play with, so that he gets a lot of exercise in stretching and reaching for things. Letting him work on his own sometimes is beneficial. You don't always have to tell or show him what to do. Giving the baby a chance to handle many new and different objects on his own is also a learning experience.

42

Play "Pop-Goes-The-Weasel" with the baby. Say the rhyme slowly and raise the baby's arm up in the air when you come to "Pop." Soon the baby will know where the "Pop" comes, and start to raise his arms by himself. This is a fun game that both you and the baby will enjoy. Just as a matter of caution though, you should not jerk the baby's arms up or swing him by them. You could very easily cause a dislocation of his arm.

Give the baby a "piggy-back" ride on your shoulders. You'll help him to gain balance and body control. The baby will also see the world from a new angle.

Show the baby that you can put a cup on the table, and then you can turn it over. Let him try. Pots and pans are good for this, too.

Let the baby ride up and down on your knee. Sing "Ride a Cock Horse" to him:

> Ride a cock horse to Banbury Cross,
> To see a fine lady upon a black horse.
> Rings on her fingers and bells on her toes,
> She shall have music wherever she goes.

Put some toys in a big box, so that the baby has to stretch and reach way in to get them.

Roll the baby up in a blanket or sheet, and then gently unroll him. See if he can play this game by himself while you watch.

Hang up some balloons and let the baby bat at them. Supervise this game carefully.

43

Place favorite toys in places where the baby has to crawl to reach them. Give the baby places to crawl in, around, and through. Give him places where he can decide to crawl over or under, between or around, or where he can pull himself up.

A new round basket or trash can make a fine toy for the baby to learn to climb or crawl on. Or you can make a tube-shaped roll from a piece of linoleum or thin aluminum. Tie it to the desired shape with rope, strong string, or wire, and then cover it with felt. Show the baby how he can use this toy to climb on, to push, to crawl into, or to push things into.

Toss a soft ball or a bean bag and let the baby crawl after it. This is a fun game for a group of babies.

If you have a beachball that you blow up yourself, inflate it until it's not quite hard enough to bounce. Put the baby on the ball on his stomach, and slowly roll him back and forth. This is a good game to help the baby develop his sense of balance. He'll enjoy it, too.

Roll a toy truck or can away, out of the baby's reach. Then ask him to go get it for you. When he brings it back, roll it again, in another direction. The baby will have fun, and may even try to roll it back to you. If he does, encourage him. But the baby may just pick it up and carry it to you. Change what you do to fit in with what he does.

44

A playpen is a good place for the baby to begin to pull himself up to a standing position. Balance a toy on the top rail. This will encourage the baby to pull himself up to reach it. Other furniture in the center is also fine for the baby to pull himself up on, provided it is heavy, sturdy, and not likely to fall over or give way.

A walker or "jump seat" will give the baby exercise for strengthening his legs and putting weight on them while not actually having to stand up by himself. This will help him coordinate the body motions necessary for rising and standing. In addition, a walker makes it possible for the baby to move about long before he can walk on his own. Don't overdo this, however. A short period in the walker each day is all that the baby needs.

When you notice that the baby can stand firmly on his feet while holding on, he can try walking. Take both of his hands and squat in front of him. The child should take a step forward if you pull him gently towards you. Be careful not to force him to do something he is not ready for. If he doesn't want to walk or seems frightened, stop and try again another time. If he does well and seems confident, the next step is to let go of one hand, helping him to balance himself with the other hand. You can also begin to increase the distance, just a little at a time, between the baby and you as he tries to walk. Be ready to comfort the baby if he falls, or praise him if he succeeds.

When the child really seems ready for walking, you can walk with him by holding both his hands and walking backwards in front of him. Try some other ways to hold him, also. You can sometimes hold him by the waist or hips, with you walking either backwards in front of, or forwards in back of the child.

45

The baby will soon become aware of stairs, and try to climb them. You'll really have to keep an eye on him now that he is moving about freely. If he finds the steps to the low sliding board, help him crawl up them, and then give him help and support to slide down if he wants to. Don't force him; let him decide.

Put chairs, pillows, boxes or stools around to make an obstacle course for the baby. Let him crawl and climb his way through to you. Greet him enthusiastically when he gets to you.

46

The baby has probably now become a toddler, and you'll find that he'll love to pull practically anything attached to a string. Give him lightweight pull toys, and they won't bang up the furniture as much. Anything that makes a noise as it is pulled is an extra bonus to the baby.

Some good things you can use to make pull-toys are old metal measuring cups; old bracelets; empty thread, typewriter or film spools; toilet paper or towel tubes; pine cones; old stuffed animals; tube-shaped ice cream cartons or small boxes. Tie several of these kinds of items on a string, knotting each one a few inches away from the next. Give the end of the string to the baby, and let him go to town.

Make a train by connecting several ice cream cartons or other boxes. You can decorate them to look like a train if you want to. Make a "creepy crawly," by alternating metal jar caps and empty spools.

If you seal a bell or a few pebbles inside the containers you put on a pull toy, they'll make lovely noises for the baby.

Try a game of hide-and-seek with the baby. Pretend you are hunting for him, and look all over, calling his name. Then you can hide, and call out to the baby something like "I'm hiding, Lizette, come see if you can find me." Keep talking until the baby finds you. At first, it will help if you leave an arm or leg sticking out so the baby can easily find you.

You should have a daily dance time with the babies. It will be fun for all of you. Play action games. Try "This is the Way We Wash Our Clothes," (tune of "Here We Go 'Round the Mulberry Bush"). Vary the activities mentioned in the song. You can sing "This is the way we take a walk . . . walk around . . . march around . . . drive the car . . . run to school . . . dance together . . . rock the baby . . ." and so on. You'll think of lots of things.

47

The baby enjoys a lot of movement and action now, so keep him busy and active. Block play, "Peek-a-boo," crawling, playing with pots, spoons, and other containers, and water and sand play are just a few of the activities that will keep the baby happy.

Let the baby try crawling through a hoop if you have one, or a big box or barrel. See how many times he can crawl under a board, with you lowering it each time.

GROSS MOTOR ACTIVITIES, 12—18 MONTHS

Let him crawl under tables, into boxes, or between two chairs. These kinds of activities are good to help the baby learn about how much space his body takes up when it is doing various kinds of actions.

Play a stretching and squatting game. Here's a jingle to go with it:

Up my arms go,
Now I'm tall.
Down I go,
And now I'm small.

"Ring-Around-the-Rosy" is a good group game. All the children hold hands and walk in a circle, singing this tune. When you get to the words "all fall down" which end the song, everybody squats or stoops. Another group game is "Jack-in-the-Box":

Jack is down, *(children squat)*
The lid on top.
The lid flies off,
And up he(she) pops! *(children jump up)*

48

When the baby is trying to throw the ball, he can be either sitting or standing. Sitting will be fairly easy for him, but he also needs to practice throwing while he is standing. This helps him to learn to throw and balance himself on his feet at the same time.

The baby also needs to practice picking up the ball while he is standing. Give him large balls (such as beach balls) to kick, and small balls (like tennis balls) to throw and catch.

Show the baby how to "throw kisses," if he doesn't already know how. This is good practice of the casting motion.

Fleece balls are especially good for young children to throw around. They are light, they can't hurt people or things, and they are easy to make.

HOW TO MAKE "FLEECE BALLS":

Materials: *bright-colored carpet yarn
*nylon cord
*two cardboard circles, 5″ in diameter
*scissors

Procedure: 1. Cut a 2″ hole in the center of both cardboard circles.
2. Place these two pieces of cardboard together, and wrap about three yards of yarn around the rim, through the hole. Cover the rim all the way around.
3. Wrap a second and third three-yard piece on top of the first one.
4. When you have as much yarn wrapped around as you need, insert scissors or knife between the two cardboards.
5. Cut the yarn at the outer edge of the cardboards, between the two pieces. Do *not* remove from cardboard yet.
6. Tie a piece of nylon cord down between the two pieces of cardboard around the center of the yarn, closing the center opening. Tie it around several times and knot it *very* securely.
7. Pull the yarn ball out through the center hole; trim it up if it seems shaggy.
8. Save the cardboard circles. They can be used over and over again.

Make larger-sized fleece balls for the smallest and youngest children. Talk about the balls; how they look and feel, how they sound, what you can do with them. Remember that when young children play "ball" they won't be able to really catch or throw properly. Fleece balls are good for practicing these skills, because the need to run after stray balls all the time is eliminated.

The baby needs much practice on these developmental skills, so try to provide a large variety of balls of different shapes, sizes, textures, and degrees of softness. Don't forget a large selection of bean bags, too.

With bouncing balls, the baby can develop his eye-hand coordination along with his muscular control. These activities also provide impulse control, and help develop a sense of direction.

49

Be sure that the baby has many toys he can push or pull. These kinds of toys help him to organize his behavior. He learns that when he does one thing, something else happens. For instance, he finds that when he picks up the string and walks along while pulling it, the toy duck follows him and quacks. The baby is learning sequencing behavior.

Let the baby try walking on different types of surfaces. He can walk on the grass, on the gravel, on sand, on the sidewalk, or on wooden boards. He'll enjoy these experiences.

Here's a list of other good activities that can be done indoors or outside:

pretend grocery shopping
blowing and catching bubbles
painting with water
simple singing games
flying paper airplanes or kites
dancing with gauzy scarves
acting out things with action cards

Tie some colored ribbons to two favorite toys. You might choose, for example, a toy car and a teddy bear. Put the toys in front of the baby, but out of his reach. Stretch the ribbons out so he can reach them. See if he will pick up the ribbon and pull the car or the teddy to himself. You may have to show him how, and then the baby will have a wonderful time. Use different toys the next time you play this game.

50

Now the baby has to be given a chance to develop complicated motor planning such as running, stopping, turning corners, etc. He's at the developmental level when gross motor activity takes the lead over fine motor activity. You may find that he runs, but stiffly. He may be pretty good at starting and stopping, but cannot turn corners or walk backwards as well. So he needs practice in all of this. Try to let him run around and explore his environment with as few restrictions as possible, both indoors and outside.

When the baby is doing all of these things, talk about what he is doing. Say, for example, "Gracious, Chester, look how fast you can run. Let's see if you can run backwards now."

Use a short ramp on a sliding board to help the baby slide down on his back, and then on his stomach. Let him try going head first and then feet first. Always stay with him as he tries these activities, but let him do as much as he safely can on his own.

In the winter, a wooden crate (if you can get one) makes a good sled. Attach a rope and pull the baby down the sidewalk or around the yard.

In the fall, you can rake piles of leaves together for the children to play in. If there are no leaves around, maybe you could bring in large plastic bags of them from somewhere else. Dump them out, and use a bamboo rake to keep piling them up and over the children as they flop in them. Perhaps you could also do this in the park. They will have a terrific time.

The baby will enjoy toys that rock or sway while he is on them, as long as he can control the speed and motion. Rocking chairs, rocking boats, rocking horses, etc. are all very pleasing to him.

You may think all of these activities are "just play," but they are very important to the baby. He must learn to handle his own body, and to find out what kinds of effects he can make on the things in his world. So he tests himself against these things, and learns about both. His method may be play, very active play, but he is really learning and accomplishing.

51

When the baby uses a plastic or wooden hammer with a pounding bench, he is developing arm and shoulder muscles, and also eye-hand coordination. You'll notice his improvement. At first, he'll use his whole arm to pound, but as he gains control, he'll begin to use just his wrist. Make sure that the pegs are loose enough in their holes for him to hammer them through to the other side. Then show him how to turn the bench over and start again.

Play or sing some music and let the baby beat on a pot or pie plate with a wooden spoon. You can help if you'll clap the rhythm for him. Learning to beat out a rhythm is important, so play records or sing songs with different tempos and rhythms. Remember to talk about what you are doing.

52

The baby can begin to do many more complex activities. He'll want to try climbing steps, using jungle gyms, crawling through tunnels, climbing on rocks and piles of dirt, and walking and climbing on uneven surfaces.

Try to provide the baby with chances to do these things, because this will help him develop better balance, motor planning and control, and help him understand about his own body in relation to space.

See how many activities you can think of to help the baby to get to know about the world. Give him a chance to learn how to handle equipment. Let him turn the radio or television off or on. Let him put the light on, turn the spigot off, or flush the toilet.

Send the baby on errands for you. Make a game of asking him to go get a toy or other object for you, or to put something away for you. You may find that the baby can be really helpful to you if you let him. As you are working, also try to think of ways he can help you push or pull something.

53

Show the baby that when you drop a ball, it will bounce up and down on the floor. Then let him try it. Show him that if he throws it hard at the floor, it will bounce high. Let him experiment with trying to bounce and catch the ball. The best kind of ball for these kinds of activities is a beach ball or a basketball.

Let the baby try a smaller ball when he has had a lot of practice with the larger ball. He'll quickly learn that if he opens his hands, the ball will fall. Then he'll learn that he can swing his arm as he drops the ball, so that it will roll, bounce or fly through the air. When he can do these two simple motions, he is on his way to playing all kinds of ball games.

Put a large box or basket on the floor and let the children toss objects into it from various distances and heights. Another thing you can do is to lay a box on its side and let the children try to kick the ball into it. To help strengthen the baby's leg muscles, show him how to jump with both feet off the ground. This is also good for the baby's sense of balance.

Help the baby by holding one or both of his hands as he tries to walk up or down steps, jump off steps, and jump over objects. Gradually he won't need you to hold his hand, but he may still want you near to boost his confidence.

Let the baby use a sturdy box or a step-stool to get something he wants. In this way, he will learn about height, as well as get practice in climbing.

To help the baby learn about direction and space, let him explore and talk to him about what he explores. Tell the child he is climbing up, crawling through, swinging higher, sliding down, hiding, or running.

55

Give the baby many opportunities to crawl, jump, roll, hop, or walk to certain spots. Let him become aware of where he is, when he is to go, and where he has been. This strengthens his concepts of directionality.

Give the baby the large muscle exercise that is essential to this level of his development. Let him experience the relationships between words like "run," "hop," and his actions. This is how he will learn the meanings of these words. You can demonstrate. Say a word, such as "hop," and then let him try. He'll become more and more familiar with the concept of an action word.

Play the "mirror" game. Stand in front of the baby and have him try to copy all of your actions. After a while you can switch around, and you can copy his actions.

Help the baby learn to walk forward and backwards, balance on one foot, walk tip toe, lie on his back and "pedal" in the air, turn around, jump over something or down from something. All of these are good for balance.

A toy on which the baby can sit and push himself is great for strengthening legs.

56

Have the baby walk on a narrow strip of carpet or between taped lines. You can include these activities with others, such as climbing over or crawling through boxes and barrels, and have an obstacle course. Some of these activities may be good for the baby to try with his eyes closed. This is excellent for balance. Let the baby pretend he is a cat walking on an imaginary fence. Let the baby pull himself along the floor on a wide board on his stomach. This is reinforcing to his sense of balance, and he'll think it's great fun.

Most activity now will be walking, running, climbing, carrying, etc. This is a very active developmental level, and the baby is now capable of thinking of and carrying out his own activities.

Be sure he spends time both indoors and out in self-planned play. A wagon is a good toy, for the baby can lean on it, pull it, or fill it with toys and other items. Toys that have handles or strings for pushing or pulling are also fine for him at this time.

Encourage the baby to try pushing fairly heavy objects, such as a chair, or a large box. Make sure it isn't too heavy for him.

The baby loves to run, and he will love it even more if you chase him. But turnabout is fair play—let him chase you, too.

58

Play rattle games with the baby. Make him work to see a rattle you are shaking. As you do this, try to keep almost out of the baby's sight. He will have to listen for the sound rather than look at you. Shake the rattle a little behind his head. If he looks up but still doesn't see it, move it until he can see it, and then move it back out of sight again. Keep doing this until he moves his head and tries to see it. When you're sure he sees it, ask him "Can you see it now, Sammy?" Do this on both sides of his head. If he reaches for the rattle, let him play with it. Repeat this game again later.

You can play another rattle game with the baby while he is lying on his stomach. Dangle the rattle in front of his face, and then slowly raise it so he has to raise his head to see it. You can also show him how to push his body up with his arms so he won't lose sight of the rattle. Lower the rattle and start over.

Crumple paper in various places near the baby's head. Encourage him to listen.

Whisper in the baby's ears, first on one side and then on the other. See if he'll respond by turning his head towards the ear you are whispering in.

If you hang a wind chime where the baby can both see and hear it, he will enjoy trying to connect the pleasant sound with the fascinating object he sees dangling and swaying overhead. Be sure he can't reach it.

59

"Peek-a-boo" games are fun for the baby, and they help him to look around at all the things he can see. During "Peek-a-boo" he'll see your face in many different ways, and this will interest him in looking and learning.

Keep the baby supplied with many different things to look at. Hang pictures and toys on a nearby wall where he can see them.

Let the baby look in a mirror. If you have a hand mirror, you can both sit down and be comfortable. Say to the baby, "Look, I can see Mary in the mirror," or "I can see Della here on my lap, and here in the mirror." Always use the child's name when you talk to him. Not only will he learn his own name that way, but he will feel more important. Let the baby point to himself in the mirror. If you do this often enough, the baby will begin to recognize himself and what he looks like.

You can also show the baby what his favorite toy looks like in the mirror. See if he reaches toward the mirror, or reaches for the real toy. If he doesn't seem interested in the mirror, let him have the toy to play with and try again later. Be sure not to tease him. Remember to always play this game *with* the baby. Never leave the baby alone with a mirror that might break.

Hang a merry-go-round mobile over the baby's crib. He'll watch it and try to reach for it.

HOW TO MAKE A MERRY-GO-ROUND MOBILE:

Materials:
*paper plate
*ribbon
*cardboard
*scissors
*felt markers

Procedure:
1. Color wedge shapes (like pie slices) in an "every other" pattern on the paper plate.
2. Cut animal shapes from cardboard, and color them.
3. Punch holes in the rim of the plate, and in the center of the animals.
4. Cut ribbons into six-inch pieces.
5. Run ribbons through each of the rim holes on plate, and fasten securely.
6. Run the other ends of the ribbons through the animals, and fasten securely.
7. Tie a ribbon through the center of the plate and hang the mobile over the baby's crib.
8. Make sure the baby cannot reach the mobile, for safety's sake.

Sometimes you can try screening the mobile, so that it will move in and out of the baby's sight.

Move toys up, down and around in front of the baby's eyes. Make him move his head to follow it. If the baby tries to grab the toy, let him have it. He's interested in looking at it more closely. Move it out of his sight sometimes, and then bring it back. Try to keep him looking for it.

Tie a string to an embroidery hoop or a favorite toy and place it so the baby can't reach it. Give him the end of the string and show him how to pull it to get to the toy. For the sake of safety, don't leave the baby alone with this toy.

Have the baby watch while you slide a rag doll across the table until it falls off. See if he starts to look down at the floor before the doll falls off.

61

Make a busy-box for the baby. Get some simple household objects, and fasten them securely to a smoothly sanded and painted board. You can use a door knob, a light switch, a roller skate wheel, a door bolt, a cabinet latch, a screen door hook, and other kinds of gadgets. You'll find that the baby will spend a long time playing with this board, trying to make all the gadgets work.

Give the baby toys that let him use his sense of touch. Let him feel satin, terry towels, waxed paper, sandpaper, and many other things that you'll think of. Just be sure that they are safe for him to touch and to put in his mouth.

The baby would probably also like a soft spongy ball, a rag doll, or even a clean spoon to hold and feel and put in his mouth.

Take the baby for a walk outdoors, and let him feel brick, the porch rails, the sidewalk, and many other things that you and he can find outside.

While outdoors, the baby will enjoy rolling around on a blanket, and feeling all the parts of his body while it touches the ground. Let him do this inside too.

Here are some things that the baby will enjoy: putting his hand in a paper cup or empty kleenex box, listening to the sound of squeeze toys as you press them against his tummy or face, crawling all over you while you sit on the floor, watching you clap and trying to do it himself.

Rub the baby's arms and legs with different kinds of cloth so he can notice the difference in the way they feel. You can try velvet, wool, burlap, and many other kinds of cloth.

62

Here's a good game to play with the baby: move bright objects in every direction about fifteen inches in front of his face. Play stop and start games with the object. Move and shake a colorful object rapidly in front of him, then stop it suddenly. Then start over, going up and down, back and forth, and around and around. Stop it again. These sudden stops and starts will surprise the baby and keep him interested.

Try moving just your hands in front of the baby's face, or just open and close them so he can see them.

Try sitting on the floor or at a table with the baby in your lap. Put a piece of string on the table, and let him try to pick it up and pull it toward himself. When he has played this game for a while, put a string with a toy tied to it along side the first string, and let him see what happens when he pulls this new string. Let him find out for himself that only the one string has a toy on the other end.

Now you can try to teach him to always pull the right string. Put the string in front of him so that he can see that the toy and the string are connected. Then ask him to get the toy. At first he probably will want to play with the string, but then he'll spot the toy. He still may not know that they are connected, but as he "experiments" he will at last pull the string to get the toy.

63

Show the baby how he can turn a plastic cup upside down, and then right side up again. Let him find out for himself that he must turn a toy with wheels right side up before it will move.

Make a happy face on one side of a paper plate, and a sad face on the other side. Move the plate puppet back and forth in front of the baby. Show him the sad side, and then the happy side. He will be interested, and may even begin to talk to it. When he reaches for it, let him have it to play with and discover what he can see on both sides.

Try holding the baby's favorite toy or doll upside down. See what his reaction is.

64

As the baby grows better at grasping, place a toy near his hand so that he must reach out and grasp it himself. Provide many different toys and objects of many textures, shapes and materials. Let him become familiar with the sounds they make as you shake them, set them down, etc.

Give the baby several small rubber balls to try to pick up. Now that the baby is starting to use his thumb when picking things up, it is important to give him many opportunities to practice this new skill.

Give the baby a large rag doll, and let him move the legs up and down. Talk to him about it and about what he is doing with it.

HOW TO MAKE A RAG DOLL:

Materials:
*fabric
*foam stuffing
*newspaper
*yarn
*felt
*scissors
*pins
*needle and thread

Procedure:
1. Make patterns out of newspaper, in the size you want, for the body shape and for the head, arms, and legs.
2. Pin patterns to fabric that is folded double, and cut out two body shapes (front and back), two head shapes, and two pieces for each arm and each leg.
3. Sew the body and head parts together, leaving openings in each for stuffing.
4. Sew arm and leg parts together, turn right side out and stuff.
5. Turn, stuff, and finish sewing body and head.
6. Sew head, arms and legs to body.
7. Sew on felt pieces cut in the proper shapes for the face. Sew on yarn for hair. Use your imagination and make the doll have as cute or as funny a face as you like.

Another toy you can make for the baby to play with and examine is a turntable of pictures.

HOW TO MAKE A TURNTABLE OF PICTURES:

Materials:
*small plastic kitchen turntable
*pictures from a magazine or book
*glue (non-toxic)
*clear contact paper

Procedure:
1. Glue simple, colorful pictures around the top of the turntable.
2. Cover the pictures with clear contact paper.
3. Show the baby how to turn the table to make the pictures move.

APPLE TREE ACADEMIES, INC.
PO BOX 4206
GREENSBORO, NC 27404

The best way the baby can learn about things is to play with them himself, and watch them change. Encourage active playing and discovering.

Give the baby a piece of paper to crumple, uncrumple and crumple up again, so he can see how it changes its shape and the way it looks and feels. Let him try cellophane, tissue, foil, etc.

Roll a ball to him, so he can see it roll. Let him try to roll it himself, too.

Wind a length of brightly colored ribbon around your finger, and let the baby pull on the loose end of it. He'll see that as he pulls, the ribbon will change its shape into a long string. Don't leave the baby alone with the ribbon, because he may try to eat it.

Show the baby some large pop-beads hooked together, and then pull them apart. Hold the two sections a few inches from each other. The baby may look from one section to the other as if trying to remember how they looked before, when they were connected. After a while, put them back together while he is still watching. Let the baby have them to play with and explore, if they are large enough that he cannot swallow them.

65

If you hang a mobile over his crib or playpen, the baby will watch it and try to reach for it. For a change you can hang a piece of elastic across his crib. Hang different objects from it, such as crushed aluminum foil, colored plastic measuring spoons and cups, and bright pieces of paper cut in interesting shapes. For instance, cut a piece of paper in a spiral, then fasten it to the elastic by one end, letting the spiral dangle down in front of the baby.

Put a toy on a pillow so that the baby can reach the pillow, but not the toy. See if he will pull the pillow towards himself. Next, hold the toy above the pillow. Will he still pull the pillow to get the toy, or will he reach straight for the toy?

Sit on the floor with the baby. Take one of his favorite toys and place it on a blanket that he can reach to pull. Then put both toy and blanket a little out of his reach. When he crawls over to grab the blanket, say "That's it, Doug, pull the blanket, and then you can get the toy."

The baby will enjoy rhythm games and fingerplays that you and he can play together. Use the rhymes below, or use other songs that may have been handed down in your family and/or culture, so as to carry on whatever is special to the child.

Here are some ideas for ethnic rhymes and songs. You can probably find many more:

> Hop, old squirrel
> ei-dle-dum, ei-dle-dum.
> *(repeat rhythmically)*
> > - Black folk rhyme/song

Have the children use the names of other animals in this rhyme—use appropriate motions to accompany the rhyme.

> Oh, come along, oh, come along,
> Let's sing our Monday marching song.
> It's lots of fun to be here together,
> As we sing and march along.
> > - Black marching song

Sing this to the tune of "When the Saints Come Marching In." You can change the day of the week to suit yourself.

Try the "Mexican Hat Dance" or "La Cucaracha" with the children. Make up your own steps if you don't know them. Many versions of these Hispanic songs are available on records.

Don't forget the child of any nationality that you may have in your center. Do a little searching, and find things to talk about and sing that apply to his heritage. Maybe you'll find that one of your best sources of information can be the child's parents or relatives. Ask them. They'll probably be pleased.

Many songs are available on records, but remember that the baby's first experiences with songs are much better when they are learned and sung with you. He'll enjoy the records later, but he needs that togetherness with you. He may even want to go on with them after you are bored, but try to keep on with it as long as he is interested. After all, it is *his* learning that is our goal. Use many actions as you sing with the baby, and encourage him to try to imitate you. Here are some simple rhythm songs or games:

This little piggy went to market,
This little piggy stayed home,
This little piggy had roast beef,
This little piggy has none,
And this little pig said, "Wee, wee, wee"
All the way home.

Here is the beehive. Where are the bees?
Hidden away where nobody sees.
Soon they come creeping out of the hive -
One, Two, Three, Four, Five.
(For this one, fold your hands so your fingers are hidden, and then let your fingers pop out one at a time. This is a counting game, but don't expect the baby to count. You simply want to expose him to the rhythm and to order.)

Play "Follow-the-leader" with the baby. Try blinking your eyes, clapping your hands, or blowing a kiss. Use your imagination and you'll think of lots of things for the baby to imitate.

Here's another hand-clapping game to play with the baby. Clap his hands together with yours, and then hide them under a blanket. Here's a rhyme that can go with this game:

Clap your hands, one, two, three
Play a clapping game with me.
Now your hands have gone away,
Find your hands so we can play.

Show the baby that you can place two or three blocks in a line on the floor, and then push them along. When the baby tries, he'll see that if he pushes on the one end, the other two blocks will soon start to get crooked. This will be interesting to him, and he'll keep trying to push the blocks in a straight line like you do. (Maybe you'd better practice this yourself first.) After a while the baby may be able to do it as well as you can. Leave the blocks handy for him to play with, and give him more blocks to play with as you see he is using them more skillfully.

Try hitting two blocks together, and then let the baby have a turn.

While the baby is watching you, build a tower. Build it far enough away from him so that he can see the whole tower. Take it down, piece by piece, and place the blocks in a line on the floor. Then do it again for him. The baby will be anxious to try his hand at this, but don't expect him to be successful. The important part is for him to try. He has to practice playing and building with them before he can use them to good effect. *(See Activity #17 for HOW TO MAKE A BLOCK SET.)*

Using soft blocks as well as hard blocks with the baby will help him to learn about hard and soft.

For a baby younger than six months, out of sight is out of mind. But now the baby can begin to learn that things are still there even when he can't see them. This is called "object permanence." Learning this will help the baby know that he can depend on things even when he can't see them. He needs to know this as a beginning for his intellectual development. It's true that facts like this seem obvious to us, but we didn't always know them. We had to learn just like the baby does. These beginning rules about how things work in this world are important for the baby to know. Your job is to let the baby find out about these rules himself. You should try to provide ways for him to find out about them.

Here is a simple game using a toy and a blanket. Attract the baby's attention to the toy, and then only partly hide it under the blanket. Make sure he can still see some of the toy. Ask the baby "Where's the toy, Marcie? Can you find it?" If the baby seems unsure, show him how to find it. If he doesn't seem at all interested, keep on playing the game by yourself, but where he can still see you. If the baby finally does get interested, keep playing with him until he can find the toy himself.

Now you can try hiding the toy completely under the blanket, but make sure that he can see that there is something under the blanket. To get his attention, try moving the toy around under the blanket, and then stop suddenly. See if he will try to get it. Encourage the baby to lift the blanket to find his toy. Keep this up as long as the baby is enjoying it, and then leave him with the blanket and toy to try his own experiments on them.

You can try putting a favorite toy in a paper bag, or wrapping it in gift wrap paper. This will give the baby a little work to do as he tries to find out what is in the package. He'll probably just rip the paper the first time, but you can show him how to use his fingers to unwrap it without ruining the paper. When the child can do this, you can then make it a little harder for him by putting a rubber band around the package. After a while he may be able to wrap and unwrap his toy by himself. Don't leave him alone with the rubber band, though. He may try to eat it.

Place a soft squeaky toy under a blanket. Use the baby's hand to make it squeak. The baby will soon learn how to make it squeak all by himself.

Play "Peek-a-boo" with the baby by placing your hands over your own eyes and then over the baby's eyes. Also try placing a blanket over your head and then coming out with a "boo." The baby will take great delight in all variations of the "Peek-a-boo" game.

Place the baby's favorite toy inside a tote bag. If he is walking, he'll enjoy having the bag slung over his shoulder. If the baby is still crawling, he can pull it by the handle. This will give him another way to learn that whatever he puts in the bag is still there even though he can't see it. *(See Activity #11 for HOW TO MAKE A TOTE BAG)*

Allow the baby plenty of time to explore his environment on his own. Put boxes containing interesting things around the room. Hide toys under a low table or chest. Roll a ball under the edge of a piece of furniture, and let the baby find it there.

69

Put a toy in front of the baby, and then put a plain piece of cardboard in front of it so that he can't see the toy. Make sure the cardboard is plain and dull, so it won't seem more interesting to the baby than the toy. Let him try to get the toy himself, and he will probably try to knock the cardboard down. Show him how to reach around the cardboard to get the toy. If he seems doubtful that the toy is still there, slide the cardboard back and forth, so he can see for himself that it is. Pretty soon he'll be reaching around the cardboard to get the toy.

Now you can complicate matters for the baby by hiding the toy first in back of one cardboard, and then in back of a second cardboard, all while he is watching. Ask him to get the toy. He will probably look behind the first cardboard, because that is the first place he saw it go. When he does find the toy, act delighted and happy with what he has done. But as a word of caution, don't tease him. If he starts to get upset, stop right away and let him have his toy.

Another version of these games that teach "object permanence" is to place one of the baby's favorite toys in a box, and put the lid on it so he can no longer see the toy. Be sure that the box opens easily. This game is a little different from hiding the toy under a blanket, because the shape of the box doesn't give away the fact that there is something inside it. Getting the toy out of the box will make the baby work harder.

Follow this up by putting the toy first in one box and then in a second box. Let him see what you are doing, and then see if he can find it on his first try. Again, may we caution you not to tease or frustrate the baby. If he gets upset, let him have his toy, and try these games again another time.

When the baby is putting his toys away, play a little game with him by asking him where a certain toy is, and then let him find it and show it to you.

70

Always remember that your approval of his achievements is very important to the baby. He needs to know that he should be proud of his efforts, and that you are proud of all his skills and knowledge. It makes his efforts seem worthwhile to him. He'll enjoy learning, and know that he can. Remember too, to encourage all his efforts, not just the ones that are successful.

You can play a game of "Follow-the-leader" with the baby by using simple motions. Bang on the floor with your hand or foot, make a fist and shake it, stand up and sit down, or perform many other actions you'll think of that the baby can imitate. Talk to him about what you are doing, and when the baby imitates you, laugh with him and let him do it over and over again. You and he can both have great fun doing these kinds of things.

Ask the baby to help you tidy up by putting toys away. When he does, reward him with laughter and praise. Be sure to keep this time and other times when you work together short and sweet, but frequent.

Now you can begin to teach the baby about "one" and "many." You can say, for example, "Look, Dolly, this is one block, and here is a pile of many blocks."

Cut a square hole in the top of a shoe box. Show the baby how a block will fit through the hole, and drop into the box. When he becomes good at this, cut a round hole for an empty spool to drop through. The baby will enjoy trying to get these objects out of the box again.

You can help the baby learn about sizes by pointing out that one cookie is big, and another is little. This is a handy game at snack time. Point out the different sizes of books, blocks, toys, or people.

Put two different sized objects of the same shape in front of the baby, and ask him to give you the big one or the small one. Try this with blocks, for instance. Show him how to do it first, and don't expect the baby to get it right the first time. He will soon, if you don't allow him to become frustrated.

Help the baby to learn about what is more and what is less by placing things such as toy trucks or dolls, in groups in front of him. Show him which group has more and which has less. Eventually he will be able to tell you.

Paste pictures of small objects in plastic containers. Give the baby the small objects that match the pictures, and let him place them in their proper container. Some objects you could use for this game are tiny cars or trucks, a small plastic spoon, a doll's cup, etc. You'll be able of think of more.

Take the baby outside when it is sunny and show him his shadow. Let him move and watch what his shadow does. Move and let him watch your shadow. You can jump on his shadow, and let the child run and jump on yours.

When the baby finds something that seems interesting to him, whether inside or outside, take the time to talk to him about it. Let him know that you are interested in his discoveries. This will keep him interested in observing and exploring his surroundings.

Give the baby plastic containers to fill with water and then pour out again. Water play can be done in sinks, swimming pools, tubs, or water tables. It can also be done inside or outside. Water play is important to the baby's development of muscular control, and also to his intellectual abilities. Another thing it is good for is to relax tension. Try to give the baby the opportunity to play with water as often as you can.

If at all possible, try to set aside a quiet area especially for books and pictures. Make this a relaxing place, where you and the baby can get together in a close, one-to-one relationship. Reading with the baby is very important at this age. Point out pictures of things that the baby is familiar with, and name them. Read the book over with the baby, as you hold him in your arms. The baby needs these reading experiences with words in order to learn to talk.

Look at a magazine with the baby. Try to choose one with many colorful and interesting pictures. Show him how to hold it and turn the pages, but let him look at it any way he wants to. He may hold it right side up or upside down; he may turn one page at a time, but more likely will turn several pages at a time. Don't discourage him, and don't be disturbed if the magazine is torn.

When you and the baby are reading a book together, don't worry about the story. Just let him point to the pictures. You can tell him about them, and what is happening in them. He may enjoy pointing to the same picture over and over again. He also may call many things by the same name. For example, he may call every animal he sees a dog. Don't let this bother you. As he hears you calling things by their right names, he will soon be calling them by their right names also. He may even try to pick up the pictures from the page. He still doesn't realize that the picture is not the real thing, but this is the way he will learn.

Homemade books may easily become the baby's favorites, particularly if you make them with different materials like cotton, wool, leather, and denim, so that the baby can feel the pictures.

HOW TO MAKE A "SQUEAK BOOK":

Materials: *two pieces of fabric (preferably denim), 12″ by 20″
*four "squeak" devices (either purchased, or from a discarded toy)
*various fabrics, such as leather and those with fuzzy or napped surfaces
*needle and thread

Procedure: 1. Place one piece of denim over the other, and sew seam down center.
2. Cut leather or fuzzy fabric in animal shapes.
3. Sew animals on pages of book, with squeak devices sewn in under one or more of the animals.

73

Put a tiny object in a match box. Help the baby learn how to push the little drawer out of the box to get the object out. Both show and tell the baby how to do this. When he can do it, ask him to hide the object in the box for you to find. When he sees how the whole thing works, let him play with it alone. He'll enjoy putting it in and taking it out over and over again, and at the same time he'll be learning in yet another way that something hasn't disappeared forever just because he can't see it. You should be sure that the object is too big for the baby to swallow before you let him play this game by himself.

Get some boxes of two different shapes, perhaps two round ones and one square one. Cover all three of them with the same kind of contact paper. Seal some corn meal or rice inside the square box. Shake them for the baby; then see if he can learn to always pick the square one to shake and make a noise.

You can use juice cans for a similar activity. Fill some of the cans with corn meal or rice and leave some empty. Seal all of the cans at both ends. Paint those with corn meal or rice one color, and the empty cans another color. (Be sure to use non-toxic paint.) Pretty soon the baby will be able to tell which color cans make the noise.

Place the baby across from you at a table or on the floor. In front of you, put two or three shoe boxes and a ball. While the baby watches, hide the ball under one of the boxes, and then ask him to find the ball and give it to you. Then try hiding the ball first under one box, and then under another, while the baby is again watching you. Does he still look under the first box, or has he learned to look where he last saw you put the ball? Maybe the baby would like to hide the ball for you and let you find it.

74

When the baby is old enough to direct his own actions and understand what you say, he can begin to learn to follow directions. Help him by making gestures so he'll know what you mean. For instance, wave your hand or blow a kiss when you are asking him to say goodbye to mommy or daddy.

Some simple directions a young child can follow are "Come to me," "No," and "Give it to me." You'll find others that he can understand too. When you are saying these things to him, show him with your motions exactly what you want him to do. Beckon with your finger for "Come to me" and so forth. Remember you may have to go over these directions many times before the baby will understand what you mean and remember it. The child won't get it right the first time, and he won't always be able to do it, even if he was able to do it in the past.

As the baby goes about his explorations, he will probably start to do some things that must be stopped by a "No." But the meaning that the baby connects with "no" can have long-lasting effects. If the baby hears "no" too often, he may think that he is not allowed to do anything. He may stop his explorations and stop learning. You have the difficult job of finding a balance between helping the baby learn the rules, and yet not discourage him from exploring and learning about things.

75

Now that the baby has had many experiences with hiding games, he's ready to enjoy a new game. In this game, the size of the can is the important clue. Using three cans of different sizes, let the baby see you place a toy under one of them. Then shuffle the cans around and see if he can guess which one the toy is under. If the baby points to the wrong can, lift it, and show him that the toy is not under that one. Keep talking about what is happening. When he does point to the right can, join in his delight.

When the baby can find the right can after he has seen you put the toy under one, make it more difficult by asking the baby to close his eyes and not peek. Put the toy under the largest can every time until he always points to it. After this, vary the game by putting the toy under the smallest can every time. See if he still catches on. Don't make these games too hard for the baby, and most important of all, don't tease him. If he seems to be getting frustrated and upset, stop and let him play with the cans and the toy himself if he wants to. Maybe he would rather hide the toy and let you find it.

Another game that is fun is playing hide-and-seek with a loudly ticking alarm clock or a pocket radio. In this game, the baby has to find the object by listening for the sound.

76

Be patient with the baby when he is trying to communicate with you. His language skills are not very well developed, and sometimes you may have a hard time figuring out what he wants or is trying to say. Remember that the baby can communicate many feelings without words, and also tries to use motions, particularly pointing, to tell you his needs. He may become very frustrated, so it's up to you to become sensitive and understanding of his needs and what he is trying to say. The more the baby tries to talk and meets with success and understanding, the more confidence and knowledge he will have about his own speech. All through his second year he'll continue to discover more, and sometimes this will be very charming. At other times he may be difficult to deal with as he asserts his independence.

If you are busy when the baby asks for something, you can say "In a minute, Ellie," or "Just a moment, Steve" and then go to the child as soon as you possibly can and ask what he wanted. In this way he will learn how to behave by your good example. He'll also learn "time" words, and that sometimes he will have to wait for what he wants.

Encourage the baby to speak for himself by asking him to name familiar objects such as his bottle or his shoe. Try to let the child make a few decisions, too, about things that concern him. He can decide if he wants a cracker or a pretzel, which toy he wants to play with, and other simple and easy decisions like these. *(See section on language development for other suggestions.)*

Let the baby look in a mirror while you talk about his arm or his other body parts. While he watches, you can comb his hair, tell him to wave "bye-bye" and so forth. Tell the baby to touch his hair or face, etc. while he is looking at himself in the mirror.

Ask the baby to point to different body parts such as his head or his foot. You can vary this activity in many ways and each child will have his own special and favorite way to play it.

Let the baby point to parts of your body, and then see if he can find the same parts on a doll or on a large picture of a person.

This is a good game for two children and you. Ask each child to point to different parts of the other child's body. Point to a part of your own or a child's body and ask them to name it. This way the baby will hear both you and another child say the names of those body parts.

When dressing the child, hold up his socks and say, "Socks go on your feet, Harry. Show me your feet." You can also do this with other body parts as you are dressing the baby.

Play the game "I wiggle" with the baby. Here's how it goes:

> I wiggle my fingers,
> I wiggle my toes,
> I wiggle my shoulders,
> I wiggle my nose,
>
> Now no more wiggles
> Are left in me,
> So I will be still,
> As still as I can be.

78

Make a felt board by pasting a colorful piece of felt on a piece of heavy cardboard. Cut out shapes (for example, circles and squares) from scraps of felt, flannel, or velveteen. Let the child try to match shapes. Leave him alone to play with the shapes and the felt board. This is good unsupervised play and will make no mess to clean up.

The baby will learn about shape and size not only because every day he will see things that are square or round (or big or little, or short or tall), but because he will also hear people talking about size and shape. No matter where you are or what you are doing, you should talk about the shape and size of things around you so the baby can hear. Compare objects and people (you and the baby himself, perhaps). Let him experiment with shape and size. Let him put small things in bigger things. Let him try to put round blocks in small holes.

Make a round hole in the lid of a plastic ice cream container. Make the hole big enough for a rubber ball to fit through. The baby will enjoy hearing the ball drop in and working to get it out. Make a square hole in another container big enough for a block to fit in. Let the baby play the same way with this. Don't stop him if he tries to place the wrong object in the hole. Let him learn what fits where for himself.

79

Try to involve the baby in your daily activities as much as possible, by telling him what things are called and what they are for. Let him help you by bringing you things and finding things for you. Remember that although he may not be able to do things as well as you can, all of these activities are learning experiences for him.

When you look at books, magazines, etc., be sure to point out familiar objects and name them. The baby may be able to point to pictures of things that he is not able to name yet. You should also point out and name objects that are not familiar to him, because this is the way he will learn about them. Strengthen experience for him by showing him real objects that are the same as the ones he sees in a book.

80

The environment should be designed so that it is easy for the baby to take care of his own needs, for example, to feed himself and to keep his own personal possessions in his own place. This way he can get things for himself.

As the baby carries out various explorations, he is increasing his understanding of the space around him, and the objects within that space. He will learn to get from one room to another, and how to hunt for somebody or something. Now is the time when the baby is carrying on extended explorations of his surroundings and attaching meaning to the things he finds in terms of their use and their user. These meanings will still be very simple—the towel is to dry your hands with, the toilet is to flush. It's up to you, the caregiver, to give him every opportunity to do this learning process of exploration and discovery.

81

To help the baby find familiar pictures in picture books, ask him to show you things by asking for them by name. If he points to the correct picture, praise him, and say the name of the object again as he points. This will make him feel good and know that he has accomplished something successfully. You can point out, too, the names of objects that he may not be familiar with, so that he can learn about them also.

You may want to mark pages in some way so that you can find things that you know the baby can recognize. It's important that you are sure that the baby can point out things he is already familiar with before you move on to new and unfamiliar ones.

Pictures in books are important, because they give the baby a chance to relate what he sees to himself. If he sees a picture of a foot, let him feel his own foot, or your foot. Let him see how many other feet he can point to around the room, including those on stuffed toys, and the "feet" on furniture.

82

Always remember to start with just one direction to the baby, and make sure that it is a simple one that you know he can do, such as asking him to pick up a block. Be sure not to confuse the baby with more directions than he can follow. Gradually add another direction to the first. Soon you'll be able to give him three at once.

A good time to help the baby learn to follow instructions is when you are dressing him. See if he will hand you his shoe, for instance, and talk about what you are doing, such as "Now let's put on your shoe," "Now we're going to tie the laces," and "Now you can get down and go play."

Let the baby help you by asking him to get things for you, or to do something with you or for you. Follow up the first direction with another, as long as you are sure the baby understands and can do what he is asked. Always watch to make sure that he is interested in doing what you are asking, but you will probably find that the baby will be very responsive to helping you. Always praise him and tell him how glad you are that he brought you the right things. Thank him each time.

83

When you are talking to the baby, use his name frequently. Name objects you are using with him, and describe them, such as "Isn't your doggy pink and fuzzy, Marylynne?" or "Isn't this a slippery sliding board?" Always try to speak to him in complete sentences, even though the baby may respond with a single word. Respond by saying, for example, "Yes, Lisa, this is the red truck," if the child just says "truck." Remember, he is learning to talk by listening to you and all other adults talk.

Start with just one or two things. Don't overload the baby with too many things to name. If he points to something and tries to name it, pick it up and use it, repeating its name frequently as you talk with him.

Take advantage of all his words and activities, and try to let him do most of the pointing and naming. Let the baby learn the words for all the common objects he can see you using during the day, by hearing you talk about them and by helping you. He can learn just as fast this way, and does not always need to be presented with a quiz game of naming.

84

Keep trying to involve the baby with helping you as you go about chores. Ask him to hand you the blanket, or to fold it up and put it away, to turn the faucet on or off, etc. Your behavior is very important as the baby tries to explore his world and make sense out of it. Encourage him by talking to him, giving him reasons for what you do and what you are asking him to do. Most important, *listen to him*.

Play simple games with the children. Say "Jimmy, sit down; Sharon, stand up; Tony, wave bye-bye," etc. The children will enjoy the fun and begin to learn that more than one thing can be happening at once. If you think they are ready, you can begin giving two directions, such as "Darlene, stand up and wave," etc.

Another game you can play is hiding things and asking the baby to find them. Show him how first. For example, put a favorite toy in a shoe box, and then ask him to go to the box, open it, and take out the surprise in it. If he can't do it at first, go through it with him. Don't let him get frustrated if he isn't interested or can't do it.

85

Place a favorite toy just out of reach of the child, and beside a stick. Show him how to pull the toy toward himself with the stick. Then let him try. If he can't, help the child by holding his hand over the stick and moving the toy toward him. If he is interested, gradually step back and let him try again himself.

You can make the baby a dust mop out of a stick and some string. Show him how he can mop up balls of crumpled paper with it, then let him try it. Tell him how much you appreciate his helping you to clean up.

The most popular non-toy play materials are often things with handles. With these, the baby will learn to use a handle as an extension of his hand. You'll find that he likes to sweep, mop, scoop, etc. You'll also probably find that the more difficulty he has using his tool, the more determined he'll be in trying to put it to use. This is partly because he is trying to do the things that you do, and also because he is interested in trying to make it work. But remember, when the baby uses a long-handled toy like a broom or mop, he is probably more interested in the activity than in the results he gets. Don't be surprised if he leaves crumbs, or really doesn't get good results by your standards. He is just learning to do, not learning to clean.

The easiest way to begin is by using objects of the same size, color and shape. This can be blocks, or plastic cups, or anything that the baby can manipulate safely. Give the baby one of these articles, and then put another in front of him. Ask him if he can find another thing (name it for him), just like the one he is holding. Praise him when he hands you the matching one. Now you can try placing two objects in front of him. One should be the same as the one he's holding, and the other should be very different. Gradually add more objects, until he can find one like the one he's holding from a group of three or more objects. If he is unable to find the matching object, find it for him and let him hold and manipulate both of them. Point out their "sameness." Above all, let the baby indicate to you when he has had enough of this game, and let him go on doing what he wants to do with these articles. He may just want to forget about the whole thing and go do something else.

You can encourage the baby to begin "matching" things by showing him how to group things together when he is playing. Ask him to put all the toy trucks together in one place, and all the toy autos together in another place. Or even more simply, ask him to put all the blocks in one box, and all the plastic dishes in another box.

If you give the baby a set of empty round plastic cups and a set of blocks, and let him play with them, he will eventually learn that he can put things in the cups, but not in the blocks, that the cups roll and the blocks do not, and many other important things about how they are alike, and how they are not alike.

A good idea to use at meal time once in a while is to ask the baby to eat his mixed vegetables by eating all the peas, then all the beans, etc. Praise him when he does this, but don't frustrate him by insisting if he doesn't want to do this.

Get some large spools and paint them three different colors. Then paint circles of the same three colors on a large piece of cardboard. Show the baby how you can place a spool on a circle of the same color. Let the baby try to do it.

Try drawing or pasting pictures of objects on pieces of cardboard. These can be toys, cars, a cup, a toothbrush or other familiar objects. Then give the baby a supply of the actual objects, and let him try to place the object on the matching card.

87

Place a pile of blocks or other small objects between you and the baby. Give him one block and then tell him to take "another" block. It's important here that the baby only takes one block each time you tell him to take another. Keep trying this with you taking a turn and then the baby taking a turn until he can take "another" on the first try. You may want to vary this the next time by using different objects.

When the baby is able to take "another one" from a pile of all the same objects, you can gather three objects, two of which are the same, for instance, two cars and a block. Give the baby one of the cars and ask him to then take another car. Be careful that the baby takes the car and not the block. You can keep trying this until the baby is able to discriminate "another" object that is just like the first object. Of course, you'll only do these things with the baby as long as he is interested.

Meal time is a good time for the baby and you to practice "another." Always ask the baby if he wants another cracker, or whatever is being served. If he does, let him get another by himself.

You can make up a story about "The child who always wanted another . . ." (fill in whatever you want). Then let the children act out the story by demonstrating how they take another. Give everybody a chance.

88

Always use the baby's name and describe the objects that are his personally. Say "Here, Chuckie, put on your wooly red hat" or "Melissa, your coat has a pretty plaid hood."

You can play a game with the children, by holding up a coat or some other item, and asking them "Whose is this blue and white coat?" or "Somebody come and get their red mittens."

Another game is to lay everyone's coats out, and then tell the children one by one to go get their own. Give a lot of help and encouragement, especially to the little ones who may be shy and hang back, or who are not sure.

89

Cut out a set of pictures of children, some boys and some girls, from magazines. Play with a group of children by giving each child a picture. As you give out the pictures, say things like "Jenny, you're a little girl, so here's a picture of a little girl." Another time you can use these same pictures and ask the children to pick out one that is a boy or a girl like they are.

Play a game of asking all the girls in the group to do one thing (sit, jump, etc.), and then asking all the boys to do something different. If a child makes a mistake, correct him gently, and don't continue if the children seem confused. You can always try it again later.

Talk about little boys who will grow up to be men (like the children's fathers), and little girls who will grow up to be women (like the children's mothers). If you can find any pictures of men and women with their children, look at them with the children and talk about them.

90

Look in a mirror with the child, and show him various smaller body parts, both his and your own. Name them as you do, and compare them with him. For instance, say "You have the cutest little nose, Freddy. Look how much bigger mine is." Then talk about what they do, and make them work. You might, for example, give the baby a bite of cookie, and let him watch himself chew. Chew a cookie yourself, and let him watch you. Both of you can also do it together. The baby will be delighted. See if he will try to imitate you if you wrinkle your nose. Let him try something and imitate him yourself.

A good story you can tell about chins and teeth is the "The Three Little Pigs."

When you are looking at pictures with the baby, point out the smaller body parts, and ask him to point to or work the part on his own body.

Use the "Thumbkin" rhyme to begin teaching him to count his fingers.

Thumbkin, Pointer
Middleman Big,
Sillyman, Wee Man
Rig-a-jig-jig
(Point to each finger and roll hands at end.)

Here are some other good fingerplays to use for this:

> Head knocker, eye winker,
> Nose blower, kiss thrower,
> Chin chopper chin.
>
> Two little eyes that open and close,
> Two little ears and one little nose,
> Two little cheeks and one little chin,
> Two little lips with the teeth closed in.

91

It's important for the baby to have experience with objects that he can't change. In this way he'll learn some basic facts, for example, objects can be grouped by size or shape, or even according to their use. He should also learn that things he can hold and handle (three-dimensioned objects) are related to their pictures in certain ways. He needs to find out for himself the answers to questions like "What will fit into what? In what ways are they different or the same? What can be built or done with things?"

There are many games that help the baby find the answer to these and other questions, and a few of them follow. The important thing to remember is that they are *games.* Let the child discover for himself the answers to his problems and puzzles, rather than saying "No, Patty, that's not it," or "Here, Juan, let me do it." In the beginning, you can play these games with the baby, but he will soon be able to play some of them alone if you just provide him with the materials.

Give the baby three boxes that fit inside one another. There should be a big difference in sizes, so there is lots of room for the baby to make them fit. Show him what he can do with them, and then let him try. Gradually increase the number of boxes as he becomes good at nesting them.

Turn the boxes upside down and show the baby how to build a tower, by using the biggest box on the bottom and building up to the smallest box on top.

Cut colorful pictures in half. They should be at least 8″ by 11″. Paste them on cardboard, and let the baby try to match the pieces for his first experience at a jigsaw puzzle.

Remember that all beginning puzzles should be big, bright, and simple for the child to do. Start with two or three piece puzzles, and as the baby learns to do these, promote him to puzzles with five or six pieces.

Draw or cut out some sets of pictures that are all alike but one. Mount each on cardboard. Give them to the baby and show him which one is not like the others. Ask him to give that one to you, and say "Yes, Arnold, that is the one that is different." Each time you play this game, ask for an item that is "different." Then work with "same" in the same way.

Another good idea is to cut out pictures of various categories, such as people, food, dogs, cats, etc. Have a box for each group. Play with the baby by asking him to put all of the dogs in the dog box, the food in the food box, and so forth. Leave him to work on this sorting problem by himself. At first it might be a good idea to let him work with just two categories.

A good game for this age is to blow up a balloon, and let the baby watch while you gradually let the air out and it becomes smaller and smaller. Do this several times and keep talking about the changes the baby sees. When he becomes bored, let the air out quickly and watch the balloon fly away. The baby will love this, and you'll probably find that you'll be bored before he is.

Another good game is to drop vegetable dye into some water and let the baby watch the change in color. If you can get a big transparent gallon jug, you'll be fascinated too. Don't forget to talk about what you are doing. Ask him what he sees happening.

It is important for the baby to watch and imitate things—both human and non-human things. Help him to try to imitate growing flowers or a tree swaying in the breeze. He can imitate the wind, or a kitten—use your imagination and let the child use his.

Here's a good fingerplay you can try:

> The sun comes out and shines so bright,
> *(hands over head, arms shaped in circle)*
> And then we have a shower,
> *(hands over head, fingers wiggling)*
> The little bud pushes with all its might,
> *(push fist into other hand)*
> And soon we have a flower.
> *(open both hands up and out in tulip shape)*

The baby will especially enjoy simple stories about himself and his everyday activities. Use your imagination and you can keep him interested in hearing stories about himself.

You can make a scrapbook about the baby and his life at the day care center. He will enjoy looking at and "reading" about himself and the other children.

Put some non-toxic paint in a low-sided pan, after laying a few paper towels in the bottom. This makes a stamp pad. Give each child a large sheet of paper or cloth. Cut some vegetables, like potatos or cucumbers, either in half or in slices. Show the children how to make prints on their paper by rubbing the vegetable on the pad of paint, and then printing it on the paper or cloth. Everyone will enjoy this. Some other things you can give the children to print with are keys, hair-rollers, sponges, pencils, leaves, half an orange or lemon, or a wooden spoon. You can probably find lots of other objects that will make good prints.

Children of this age love to take things apart and put them together again, and to pound and squeeze, so now is the time to give them many experiences with clay or play-dough. *(See Activity #28 for HOW TO MAKE PLAY-DOUGH)*

You can try the child now on one of the hardest skills he has to learn—cutting with scissors. Make sure you give him safe ones with rounded points, but also be sure that they really will cut and that they are not too stiff for him to work. Show him how to hold the scissors and make them work, and then let him try, using newspapers or old magazines. Watch out for frustration, and let him stop if he wants to.

Help the baby when he runs into trouble doing puzzles. Show him how to dump the pieces out on the table, and then help him to see the relationship of the piece to the place where it fits. Let him feel the edge of the piece and the edge of the space where it goes, and then see if he can slide it in place. Don't hurry him. Help and encourage him by praising him and making the problem simpler. Remember, though, the baby is doing the puzzle, not you.

You can keep the children's level of frustration down if you try explaining ahead of time what is going to happen next. Say, for instance, "Nap time in five minutes." That way they can prepare themselves for something different coming up, rather than having to be unpleasantly surprised or interrupted.

Ask the child to tell you what he was doing before he came to be with you. Children love to talk about themselves and what they are doing. In interacting with you, the child should gain a feeling of freedom to experiment and explore, and a feeling of trust in you and the environment. Let each child become aware of himself as a person.

Teach the child to repeat simple sound patterns. For example, use one tap on the table, two taps on his knee, or a short sound, and a long sound. Do it first yourself, and then let the baby try.

Keep on the look-out all the time for counting activities. Count everything, ranging in number from one to ten. Help the baby count his cookies, shoes, blocks, mittens, toys. Show him how to count his fingers. Teach him how to hold up his fingers to show how old he is. Let him stack blocks, and count them. When he looks at a picture, ask him to point to and count how many objects of one kind he sees. He probably won't learn to really count yet, but he will be beginning to develop a "number sense."

Sing counting rhymes and fingerplays with the child. "Ten Little Indians" is a good one, or you can try "One-Two Buckle My Shoe."

Here are some others you can try:

Two little dickie birds sitting on the hill,
(hands out, forefingers out)
One named Jack and the other named Jill.
Fly away, Jack. Fly away, Jill.
(pull hands back, fingers out)
Come back, Jack. Come back, Jill.
(hands out, forefingers out as beginning)

Our little baby has ten toes,
Two little ears and one little nose.

One little hand reaches out so wide,
One little hand is down by my side.

I bring my hands together to clap, clap, clap.
One and one are two hands, now resting in my lap.

Old shoes, new shoes,
Little goody, two-shoes

Put two cups on the table, with one in front of you and the other in front of the child. Now you can show him how to play "One for you and one for me." Put a small item, such as a penny or a peanut, in his cup, and then put one in your cup. Keep going like this until you have about three in each cup. Then let him try it. It will be even more interesting for him if you then increase the cups, and tell him that one cup is for him, one is for you, one is for mommy, and one is for someone else that he knows. See how far you can go with this game, with the child still able to do it. Be careful though, to notice if he is getting bored or frustrated. If he is, stop and try again later.

Try cutting the numbers 1, 2, and 3 out of sandpaper and pasting them on heavy cardboard. Tell the child the names, and let him trace their shapes. This way he can both see and feel how they are shaped.

If you think he is interested, you can teach the child to count from one to ten. That is, teach him the words, for he will not yet be able to understand what they mean. But he will know that they are words that big people use to count, and will probably enjoy learning and saying them.

94

To help the child understand and follow directions, you can play "Follow the leader." Do the actions first, and let him imitate you. Be sure to give him a turn to be the leader. Some suggested activities for "Follow the leader" are scratching on the table, drumming on the table, opening and closing the fists, bending fingers, blinking eyes, wrinkling your nose, and many others that you and the child will surely think of.

Respect the child by giving him a chance to talk and to ask questions. Don't allow him to monopolize the conversation, but be careful that you aren't either. Don't set a poor example by chattering constantly, and then refusing to listen when the child wants to talk or ask a question. Always respect him by understanding when he misunderstands and giving him a chance to get it right.

Especially during these early years, the child's emotional development cannot be separated from his intellectual growth. When he can do something, you'll see him smile or laugh, and maybe clap his hands. But when he is frustrated or scolded because he cannot perform, or even if he sees for himself that he cannot do whatever he is trying, his self-confidence is affected. So you should always treat a child with the recognition that his thoughts and feelings are interwoven.

One habit children of this age have is asking "Why?" about everything. Try asking what the child thinks before you give him the answer. This will help the child to think about things, and maybe even will cut down on those "Whys?" He may tell you instead of asking you to tell him. Encourage him to make decisions, and to express his likes and dislikes.

Listen for times during the day when the child is imitating actions and is saying or trying to say a few words. Let him imitate you as you do several simple motions one at a time. Try saying words or nonsense syllables (da di da, for instance) and let him try to repeat what you say. You can sing a small part of a familiar nursery rhyme tune, and see if he can sing it too.

Another good idea to introduce a young child to music is to let him sit on your lap, or right next to you. Clap his hands together, or let him help you bang on a drum or on the floor in a rhythmic way. You can also let him try simple body movements such as stamping his feet, marching, jumping, or swaying. Put some good lively music on the record player, or sing yourself.

The baby will want to just listen to the sound of the music, but encourage him to try some of the movements that you are showing him. If he sees you doing it, he will probably want to try it too.

Try just marching around first, and let the children follow you, clapping their hands or stamping their feet.

As the children become more adept, you can introduce them to playing drums, sticks, triangles, etc. in time to the music. But this takes a lot of concentration, and will probably take a long while before all of the children will be able to do this.

Be sure to make the children aware of the differences in the various sounds they hear. Illustrate for them loud and soft, harsh and soothing, high and low, fast and slow, etc.

Play music frequently during the day, and sing and encourage the children to sing with you. You should also provide quiet times during the day, especially when the children are awake.

When you are singing with the children, pitch your voice so that it is about the same level as the children's voices, so that they can get a good idea of how the song should sound at their voice level. This means that you will probably have to pitch your own voice higher than normal. The children will try to sing as you are singing, and if you are singing in low tones, you may find that they are singing all on one note, or straining to make their voices seem more like yours.

Gradually the baby will begin to get interested in the tiniest details. He'll explore dials, keyholes, etc. He may be especially interested in things that are broken or have missing parts. This attention to detail makes books extra attractive. Be sure to have books with lots of details.

Pictures, like words, help children remember things that have happened, especially photographs of themselves in action. They also help the children think of what is going to happen in the future.

Give the child blocks that have letters or pictures on them, and point out these interesting features so he can look at them while he plays with them.

Make a texture poster, and hang it where the children can examine it and touch it. You can just paste a variety of different textured materials (flannel, turkish toweling, etc.) on a large square of heavy cardboard, or you can make the cardboard into an interesting shape (a tree, a house, etc.) and use the different kinds of material as details of the picture.

Make a section of wall that the children can reach into a picture display area. Use large and colorful pictures with easily seen and identified features. You can put actual photographs of some of the children or staff. Talk to the children on a one-to-one basis about what they see there. Point out which picture is higher or lower than another, for instance. It would probably be a good idea to cover all of these pictures with a large sheet of transparent plastic. They'll last longer that way.

Take the children for a walk and identify different things that you see. Ask them to tell you what they see. Stop and examine some very interesting things closely, and let the children point out to you as many things about it as they can.

Perhaps, while on your walk, you will find some interesting things to take back to the center with you. If you can find some ants, spiders, or worms for instance, you can put them in a transparent container, and punch some holes in the lid, so the creatures can breathe. Add some earth and some grass or leaves, and let the children watch the movement and activities that go on day by day. If you let the children look through a magnifying glass, they'll really be able to see the details.

Make a strip story book. As you and the child turn each strip, more and more of the picture will come into view.

HOW TO MAKE A STRIP STORY BOOK:

Materials: *large spiral notebook (can be a used one)
*large and colorful pictures, approximately the same size as the notebook
*non-toxic glue

Procedure: 1. Cut the first page into three equal strips, from edge to spiral binding.
2. Glue a full page picture on the second page.
3. Cut the third page, fifth page, seventh page, etc. into three equal strips as in step one.
4. Paste a full size picture on each uncut page (the fourth page, sixth page, etc.).
5. Continue adding new pictures as you find them, as you did above.
6. Show the child the book by turning each strip to show more and more of the picture.

97

Children love short trips. Talk to them about what they will see and hear. Label objects and listen to what they say about them. Here are some suggestions for trips:

Tour of the day care center
Trip to an office building (especially exciting if somebody's parent works there)
Walk to and around in the park
Visit the post office, fire house, florist, food processing factory, printers, police station, farm, zoo, pet shop, grocery store.

When they come back, many of the children will enjoy looking at or even making books about their outing. To make a book, ask the children to tell you what they liked about the trip and write it down as they say it. Illustrate it with pictures cut from magazines, or with the children's drawings, and look at it with them. They'll particularly enjoy it if you include some pictures of them that you took while they were on their trip.

Sorting activities are useful to help the child identify various objects and their uses. The only materials you need are objects to be sorted and boxes to put them in. You can use spoons and cups, and ask the child to put things that you drink with in one box, and things you eat with in the other box. This may be difficult for him at first, and he may just want to play with the items. Let him, after you discuss what they are used for, and try again some other time to have him sort them. Use your imagination, and you'll find that you can come up with many variations of sorting games.

Remember that children of this age pay attention to only one fact about an object at a time, so ask him to sort for only one thing. You can also use these objects to let the child match identical ones, and to match objects with their pictures. Picture matching may be most difficult to do at first. It is hard for the children to understand that a picture can show what a real object looks like. Some children have trouble learning because they didn't understand this. Make sure to teach the children this. It is important for learning to read.

Begin this game by drawing or tracing an outline of a familiar object, such as a popsicle stick or even your hand or the child's hand. You can probably think of other things that you could trace an outline of. Let the child watch you while you are doing this. Let him help you hold the object in place, or even try to draw some of the line around it. Talk to him all the while about what you are doing. When you are finished, you can ask him what he thinks is underneath, and then let him see. Do this with several different objects, and then make a game of matching the objects with their pictures. Show him how to do it, and then let him try. Don't worry too much about the exact position of the object on its outline. The important thing is that the child recognizes the likeness of the object to its outline.

When the child understands the above game, you can go a little further by asking him to match objects with pictures cut from magazines. You can also switch it around. Give the child the object, and ask him to find its picture in the magazine. Then have him match pictures that are similar. They don't have to be identical—just two pictures of the same object, such as two pictures of a cat. Always remember to talk about the pictures and the objects.

When teaching this, start with the primary colors and don't use more than two to begin with. Ask the child if he wants to play a game of cards with you, just like grown-ups do. He will probably be thrilled at the idea of doing something like grown-ups. Give him two sets of cards, one colored red and the other colored blue. You can use file cards or even real playing cards. Just paint both sides in bright, non-toxic paint, or cover them with colored tape. If you are using playing cards, you can leave the backs the way they are and just cover the playing side. Let the child play with the cards for awhile, then as you pick one up, ask him to give you one just like it. As he hands you one, say "Yes, that's the blue one, Tony." If he makes a mistake, name the color he picked and ask him for another of that color. As he gets to know these colors, you can add yellow cards to the game. As with all games, only play it as long as the child is interested. This could be developed into a small group game by letting each child match his card with another child's. Let the children take turns, and say the colors as each one handles them.

You can put a red sock on the child's foot, and then show him a red and a yellow sock, and see if he can pick the one that goes with the one he has on. Don't forget to tell him the names of the colors you are using. Try to stay in the primary range at first, and pretty soon you'll find that the baby is naming the colors himself. You could try this with mittens too, or let him find someone else who is wearing something the same color as something he is wearing. Encourage him to name the colors of other things found in the center.

Make paper hats from red, yellow or blue construction paper, or use real hats if you have them in the primary colors. Then you can give the children turns wearing them, and teach them this rhyme:

> I'm two years old and like to wear
> A pretty hat upon my hair.
> Sometimes it's red (or yellow), and sometimes it's blue.
> I think I look great, don't you?

The baby will devote his particular attention to his principal caregiver, following her movements around the room with his eyes, and gazing after her in the direction she has disappeared. When you pick the baby up, extend your arms and bend down to him. If he is able to, he will try to put his arms around your neck. Perhaps you can guide his arms to go around your neck. Show your affection for him by talking to and hugging him.

Watch for times when he smiles at you or begins to reach for you as you're coming to pick him up. Be especially affectionate then, telling him how much you like to see him smile. Continually praise him as he gradually smiles more and reaches more often for you when you approach him.

When you approach the baby to pick him up, smile and speak softly to catch his attention. He will become quiet, and perhaps will try to look directly into your eyes. Then he will probably begin to coo and gurgle at you. He is trying to speak to you, so you can respond by smiling and speaking to him again.

When you are holding the baby, try to look directly at him as much as you can. Eye-to-eye contact will help the baby to focus his eyes for longer amounts of time. This is part of the child's earliest social response. Encourage him to smile at you, gently tickle his tummy or chin and when he responds, respond back to him.

Try to hold your head very close to his so he can watch your facial expressions. Show him different expressions such as a frown, a wink, opening your mouth wide, and so on. Perhaps he will try to imitate your expressions, or nod his head if you nod yours. You and he can have a good time together, responding back and forth to each other.

Play "How big is the baby—so big!," by pulling the baby's arms gently over his head. Say the baby's name when you do this with him. If you play this often enough with him, he will start to associate the game with the words, and eventually will do it by himself when he hears you say the words.

Another game that the baby will like is "Pat-a-cake." You can also play games with the baby's doll while he is watching. Try "Rock-a-bye, baby" with the doll on your knee, or "Ride-a-cock-horse"; he'll probably want you to do it with him also.

Don't forget that old favorite, "Where's Baby?," where you hide from his sight, let him find you, and then say "There he is!" Use the baby's own name.

Encourage other people at the center to show affection for the baby. They can pick him up and talk to him, and play games with him such as "Pat-a-cake" and "Peek-a-boo." In this way the baby will get to know and respond to more than just his principal caregiver at the center.

The baby may be distressed when approached by another caregiver, and cry or try to withdraw from someone who is strange to him. Of course, this depends on how familiar he is allowed to become with the others at the center. That is why it is important for the baby to get to know other people at the center. The baby should receive the kind of individual care and attention that a loving family gives him at home.

However, there is evidence that it is better for the baby if the number of adults caring for him is kept small. If he is cared for by too many people, there may be a slowing of his overall development. His human relationships must be predictable, continously focused, and consistent to produce the best results. This is possible only if a small number of adults care for any one child.

Familiar things are usually comforting to the baby when he finds himself in strange or unsettling circumstances. He may have a favorite toy or blanket that he needs to comfort himself. These should be his alone, and he should not be expected to share these "special" toys with other children, nor be teased or reprimanded about them. These items fulfill a very important function in his life. They help him to endure stressful situations long before he can talk about his feelings.

Don't be surprised when the baby suddenly cries or otherwise rejects a stranger. He is growing up, and demonstrating that he can tell the difference between a familiar and an unfamiliar face. That familiar face represents safety, comfort and pleasure to him, and he knows it well. The unfamiliar face is an unknown to him. All of us fear the unknown to a degree, and so does the baby.

Show the baby a paper bag puppet. He will be aware that it a different kind of face, but will probably be interested and fascinated with it, and not react poorly as he might to a strange face. Let him watch the puppet move back and forth in front of him, and let him try it if he wants to.

HOW TO MAKE A PAPER BAG PUPPET:

Materials:
- *paper bag
- *newspaper
- *wooden dowel
- *piece of ribbon
- *crayons or paint
- *scissors
- *yellow, red, brown, or black construction paper
- *glue

Procedure:
1. Draw or paint a face on the bag.
2. Curl colored paper strips for hair and glue on bag.
3. Stuff paper bag with newspaper.
4. Tie puppet to dowel with ribbon.

101

The baby and you can have a lot of fun with mirror games. Show him his eyes, nose, and mouth in the mirror. Then show him your eyes, etc. Let the child compare your reflection with your real face by touching and pointing.

Help him learn to identify the parts of his face by pointing to them on the baby and in the mirror while he watches. Give the name of each part as you point to it.

Wave to the baby in the mirror, and talk to his reflection. The baby will be fascinated and absorbed, and want to try this too. Give him a cracker to eat while he is looking at himself. Let him see how his mouth, teeth and tongue look when he is chewing.

An unbreakable mirror hanging over or attached to the crib will be exciting for the baby. He'll look at himself and smile, because he recognizes himself. The baby will sit in front of a long unbreakable mirror and talk to his reflection in it. When it doesn't answer, he may reach out and try to touch the baby he sees in the mirror, to find out what's the matter. Then he may perform for himself in front of the mirror and laugh out loud at the antics he sees.

Here are some rhymes you can say with the baby while you are both looking in the mirror:

Where is baby's nose?
Where are baby's eyes?
Touch the part that blows,
Now touch the part that cries.

Down-down-down go baby's fingers wee,
Reach way down and touch my knee.

Up-up-up baby's hand goes,
Reach way up and touch my nose.

102

An important development in a baby's life is the sense of power and joy he receives when he is able to influence and control the people and things around him. Show him that you will respond as soon as you can when he cries, or seems uncomfortable or unhappy.

Although the baby may not actually talk, he does learn to use his "language" for his own purposes. By the sounds he makes, he tries to find ways to call you, to keep you with him, and to call you back when you turn away. When you respond to these calls, you are teaching the baby the power of language.

Carry on conversations with the baby as many times during the day as you can. Use different tones of voice, so that he will get to know what various tones of voice indicate.

Lift the baby up high and down low, so he can watch you and others in the room from different levels, and see how things look different from different angles.

Hold out your arms to the baby as you go to pick him up. Soon he will start stretching out his arms to you when he sees you coming.

You can make the baby a happy-sad pillow. Let him see first one side and then the other. This gives him another way to notice differences in facial expressions. When he begins to show interest in both sides of the pillow, you can also make him a happy-sad plate puppet to play with.

HOW TO MAKE A HAPPY-SAD PILLOW:

Materials:
* needle and thread
* regular or pinking shears
* pieces of felt or other fabric
* foam rubber or old nylon stockings for stuffing

Procedure:
1. Cut two 8″ by 10″ pieces of fabric.
2. Cut other fabric shapes to form a happy face and a sad face.
3. Sew one face on each 8″ by 10″ fabric piece.
4. Sew the pieces together, leaving one side open.
5. Stuff the pillow through the open end.
6. Sew the open side closed.

HOW TO MAKE A HAPPY-SAD PLATE PUPPET:

Materials:
* two paper plates (plain, no design)
* felt markers
* scissors
* yarn
* non-toxic glue
* popsicle sticks

Procedure:
1. Outline eyes, nose and mouth on the inside of each paper plate. One plate should have a happy face with upturned mouth, and the other should have a sad, turned-down mouth. Use your imagination and see how good an artist you can be.
2. Sew or glue popsicle sticks to each plate for a handle.
3. Place paper plates back to back and glue or sew them together so that one side shows a happy face and one side a sad face.
4. Sew on yarn hair.
5. If you would like, you can also make different color skin shades before you draw the features. Remember, we all have different shades of skin, and we need to help the baby identify with and feel good about his own skin color.

By this time, the baby should begin to know the differences between approval and disapproval. He should react to a "no" by stopping what he is doing, even if for only a moment. You can help him by removing him from the temptation of doing something that you don't want him to do, and by letting him know gently but firmly that he is not permitted to do that. Your tone of voice will begin to remind him that he is doing something that doesn't meet with your approval.

The baby loves to watch other people. Let him watch as you and the others do routine chores around the center, and try to remember to talk to him while you work.

The baby will also enjoy listening to happy conversation between all of the caregivers and the children at the center. He might get quite excited and try to join in the conversations himself, babbling and calling to the other speakers.

"Peek-a-boo" is one of the baby's favorite games. You and he can play it often, and now you can bring in some other familiar people to the game.

Try swinging the baby to the tune of "Rock-a-bye-baby." Hold him under his arms (not by his arms), and have another caregiver hold his feet. Be gentle, and the baby will enjoy having two of you play with him.

The baby is usually a very sociable child. He'll love to visit with the other babies. The babies will begin to notice and to imitate each other. If one laughs, his playmates will laugh too, without really recognizing that he is a baby like them.

The baby should be becoming quite aware of the reactions of an audience. He will be quick to act silly or take part in a social game. You can go up to the baby and play with him, saying something like "I'm going to catch you," and get a laughing, happy response from the baby.

Comings and goings are of great interest to the baby. He likes to watch what is happening and will become quite familiar with the routines of the day care center.

Play a telephone game with the baby by pretending to talk to him on it. Then give him a turn. This way he'll learn the fun of carrying on a conversation and socializing with others.

Another social game is to pretend to give the baby's doll or teddy bear a drink. Then let the baby have the cup so he can pretend to give teddy a drink also.

Encourage the baby to go on short errands for you. For instance, ask him to take something to another caregiver. This will help the baby get to know and be sociable with others, and will also help him to feel important and independent.

The baby is growing daily more self-reliant, but interplay with other children and caregivers is still very important. The play experiences that the baby has now are laying the foundations for more structured and organized play when he gets older. As he plays "Hide-and-seek" or "Peek-a-boo" with you and others, he is learning about sequences of events, how to recognize different relationships with others, and to value the feeling of happiness that play gives to him.

APPLE TREE ACADEMIES, INC.
PO BOX 4206
GREENSBORO, NC 27404

104

A baby's personal identity development is affected by the following experiences:
1. How the baby is treated by the people close to him.
2. What he observes about the adults he admires.

Babies are very observant and sensitive. They perceive adult attitudes in behavior even though they cannot fully understand their meanings. When the baby begins to crawl, he should have the freedom to explore his environment. Make sure the area in which he crawls has been baby-proofed, both for his safety and the safety of the environment. Recognize that he cannot always be successful at what he tries, but let him try and don't downgrade his efforts.

Let the baby feel different sensations by blowing on the back of his neck or on his stomach, tickling the soles of his feet or playing with his fingers.

Use the baby's name often when you talk to him, and always use the name that he is called at home. To encourage self-identification, play such games as "Where's Juan?," or "What's Baby's Name?" Answer with his name, and he will soon be answering you himself. As he gets older, the child will start to recognize and say other people's names, and realize that they are separate from himself. It's a real step forward for the baby to recognize his own name.

Always try to interact with the baby in a way that will convey to him your dependability and good will. This is one of the most important things that the baby will learn from you in all the games you play with him. If you do this, you'll have a feeling of participating to the fullest in his growth, rather than just observing it, and enjoy a feeling of joy, love, and accomplishment.

105

The key thing is to let the baby know that his efforts are having an effect, that when he makes a sound he gets a pleasant response, or when he turns his head toward an object, he can hear, see and touch it, and perhaps even hold it. This is important not only because the baby enjoys doing these things, but because he needs to be encouraged to feel that the world is explorable, and be assured that he can make things happen. He needs to be encouraged to reach out to the world and have it respond well to him. If his early efforts are discouraged or not responded to by you as his caregiver, he may come to feel that nothing he does makes any difference.

Be careful, however, to go slowly with the baby. Don't force him to respond, or push him, or overload him. He'll tell you when he has had enough play or attention, or when he wants more. Get to know the cues he gives you, so that you can respond well to his needs.

Try to pay attention to the baby's rhythm of activities. Try not to interrupt him when he is enjoying something. Let him have the repeated experience of being able to complete the activity he is interested in, so that he may satisfy his curiousity completely about it. He will be able to develop a much longer attention span if you allow him to follow his own rhythm and interest.

Try to help the baby achieve a feeling of competence, by providing many opportunities for him to be successful in what he is trying to do. You can further his feelings of success by providing opportunities for the baby to have an effect on you. Your meaningful responses to his attempts at interaction will further his abilities to behave with intention and purpose.

Try not to be so eager to communicate with the baby that you fail to look and listen for what he may be saying or communicating with you.

106

Be sure to play slow-moving, non-threatening games with the baby. For example, you can touch the baby different places on his body, and make a sound (like "boop") each time. Watch how he smiles at each sound, waiting for you to touch him in a new place.

You can also give the baby some expressions to imitate. Try sticking out your tongue, winking your eye, smiling, etc. See if he can make the same expressions. After a while you may find that he will make expressions for you to copy.

If you do these games with one baby while sitting with a group of babies, they will all be fascinated. They will learn by watching, and from each other. But don't forget to give all the babies a turn.

Encourage the baby to play social games with others. A good one is handing a toy or other object back and forth. This is a kind of beginning conversation. The baby is saying "I'll hand you something and you can hand it back, and then we'll talk about it." Don't expect him to play this with another child, however. It works much better when played with an adult, and helps the baby to get to know and like another adult.

The kind of social games that the baby might like with other children are "Peek-a-boo" and games where they run together and chase each other.

Another fun game for you and the baby is running in place. Pretend to chase him by running in place. The baby will think this is great fun, and you'll probably find a lot of funny, personal things to try. Don't forget to try these kinds of things with a group of children.

When strangers come to meet the baby, don't try to force him to go to someone he is afraid of. Let him warm up first, and reassure him by staying with him until he begins to feel comfortable with them. Then they can try some of the games we have just suggested.

The baby may become brave enough to hand a stranger a toy, but may then change his mind and take it back. On the other hand, the baby may like a friendly stranger so much that he'll bury him with his toys. He's really inviting the stranger to talk to him. Another baby might not be that bold, but he may scatter his toys all around in front of the stranger and hope to attact his attention that way.

Many babies like to carry their "security blanket" or favorite toy with them when they meet a stranger, or a strange situation. They do this because these articles mean security to them. Let the baby have his security, and don't ridicule or tease him about it.

107

Help the baby learn to play alone. This is an important part of his development, to learn self-reliance and how to entertain himself.

When you and the baby are playing together with his toys, gradually stop playing, and just sit and watch him. Soon you should be able to get up and do something else in the room, while he plays contentedly on his own. Always provide toys that he can handle himself without becoming frustrated. Try blocks, books to look at, and other favorite toys that you know he enjoys. Remember though, not to leave the baby alone too long, so that he becomes frustrated and lonely or fretful.

Some other ideas for the baby to try "on his own" are pull toys, and toys like spoons, pans and cups that he can bang. A climbing area will interest the baby to try on his own, but be sure that it is low and safe for him to work on alone. Toys that have parts to be fitted are good, as long as you are sure he can do them without frustration. Putting things into something and dumping them out again will interest the baby for a long time.

108

The baby will increasingly be able to imitate all kinds of actions. You'll find him very good at hand movements. If you wave to him, he'll wave back to you, and of course, he loves to clap when you are clapping.

The baby will also be looking around and trying to imitate other things you are doing. He'll want a spoon when he's eating, because you are using one. He may want to try to use the spoon, and although he won't be very good at it, he needs to practice this too.

The baby will be fascinated by your actions and those of other adults he sees. Encourage him to imitate you. This is the way he learns new skills, and also builds for himself an increased sense of competence. Ask him to help you by bringing things to you or carrying them to someone else. Let him help you by placing napkins at the table, and other little jobs that he can do.

Put a block in each of your hands, and hit them together. Then let him try. Put some blocks in a container and shake it so that it makes a noise. This will delight the baby, and he will gleefully try to imitate this.

Demonstrate for him how to play "Pat-a-cake" with his doll's hands.

Play "Peek-a-boo" by ducking out of sight, then let him do the ducking out of sight.

Kiss him on the cheek, and then see if he will kiss you back.

Cough or pant like a dog, and see if he can imitate the sounds you are making. Try other sounds also.

Sniff a flower, and then let him try; take a pretend drink from a cup, and then give him the cup. See what he does.

He will enjoy imitating you rocking his doll to sleep or giving it a bottle, covering it with a blanket or wiping its nose. This is how he learns to do the things that you are doing for him and the other babies in the center.

Use old boxes, cans, pots and pans, and let the baby have a play kitchen. You might even provide him with a small plastic set of dishes and a child-sized mop and broom.

This is a good time for you to start teaching the baby to pick up his toys. Say that you are going to start picking up things, and ask him to help you. If he begins to imitate what you are doing, be sure to give praise so that to him it will be an achievement worth doing the next time.

Play games and sing songs that have actions. Good ones are "Here We Go 'Round the Mulberry Bush," "Alley Cat" or "Where is Thumbkin?." Here are some other motion fingerplays. You can make up motions and teach them to the baby.

> One little hand reaches out so wide,
> One little hand is down by my side.
> I bring my two hands together to clap,
> And then put two hands down in my lap.
>
> Here's a cup and here's a cup,
> And here's a pot of tea.
> Pour a cup and pour a cup,
> And have a drink with me.
>
> I have a jolly jumping jack,
> See how well he jumps
> Up and down, from side to side,
> He jumps and jumps and jumps.

109

The baby is now developing a greater ability to show his affections. If you hug or kiss him, he will try to do the same to you in return. Soon he will be the first to offer affection and sociability.

It is important that you share and return the baby's efforts at being sociable and affectionate. His future well-being depends on feeling wanted, worthwhile, and competently able to continue his developmental achievements.

When you play games with the baby, such as "Peek-a-boo," or any other games that you know he loves, stop at the end, and wait for the baby to tell or show you that he wants to do it again. Encourage him to tell you what he would like to do. He may want to climb up in your lap and hug or kiss you; let him. He is trying to tell you how grateful he is to you for giving him such a good time.

This human relationship that you and he are establishing is very important in the baby's healthy physical, mental and emotional development. This relationship is a powerful influence not only now, but for the future.

110

The baby has many ways of communicating without using words. When he is angry, he might scold, scowl, kick out with legs and feet or thrash his arms around. If he's happy, he'll bounce, laugh, and tumble himself around. He might coyly tilt his head to the side or drop his chin on his chest. Tugging when he wants something, and pushing away what he does not want are other actions. These are all very familiar actions and they all give a clear indication of the state of the baby's emotions.

Perhaps at the beginning of the day the baby might need help getting started, even if he is playing with something that is familiar to him. Sit down beside him, and show your interest in what he is doing. Your enthusiasm will interest and comfort him, and help him to gain experience in handling his own emotions.

Give the baby a few minutes warning that playtime is coming to an end. This will give him time to finish up.

Respect any and all promises made to the child. Unless you are sure, never say, "I PROMISE." The baby will learn to be trustworthy and keep promises by the way other people keep promises to him.

Help the baby to feel good about his sex and his color. He or she must learn that either sex is a good sex, and one is not better or worse than another. The same thing applies to skin color.

The baby loves to tear up magazines and papers. This is good for him, and he should have this opportunity often. It is a safe release for aggression and a good learning experience. Soon, with your guidance, the baby will learn what he can "go to town" on and what he cannot.

Help the baby to develop internal control, self-motivation, and self-direction. People who develop inner controls as children function better as adults. The development of these qualities does not start at five or fifteen years. It begins with the way you help the baby to learn to wait for his bottle, or stop taking another child's toys.

111

Now you can begin to give the baby increased freedom, independence, and opportunities to function on his own. But you should only do this as the baby shows you that he has the understanding and ability to do so. You may find that from time to time you will have to back up and permit less when the baby finds he can't handle a situation. This way you can help the baby to learn to handle his world without trampling on the worlds of others. Help him to begin to develop self-control, and to begin to accept responsibility for his behavior. Give explanations for "why" with your "no-no," so as to prepare him for what you and the world are going to demand of him.

Many of the baby's demands come from his desire to be like a grown-up. He'll want to talk on the telephone, pour the milk, feed himself, and do all sorts of things that he is not yet capable of doing. Although this can create problems, they are certainly a healthy sign. The baby sees himself as growing up, and entitled to grown-up privileges.

One thing to be careful of is overprotecting the baby. Two dangers involved here are: first, if you always rush to stop the baby's explorations, you might lessen or stop his desire to explore and learn; and second, he may learn to fear doing things, and lose his courage to explore.

The baby must have good environmental stimulation that is appropriate for his needs, and gives him good experiences to build on. It is important for his future development that this experience be offered as early as possible.

Remember that the baby doesn't start to develop a self-image at five, or ten. His self-image begins to develop from the moment of birth. It's important to realize that it can be easily damaged very early in the baby's life.

To gain attention and to establish his own separateness from others, the baby will begin to show his clothing and toys to everyone. It's as if he is saying "This is me, right?" He has to figure out who he is, where he fits in, and how he relates to the rest of his world.

Take a picture of each baby. Mount these pictures on the wall, behind a sheet of plastic, and let each baby pick himself out and look at all of the other pictures. Before you put them up on the wall, let each baby hold his own picture for a few seconds, and then give it to you to hang up. Talk to them about their pictures, and say their names.

Make a folding screen mirror. You can tape shirt cardboards together and cover them with aluminum foil. The baby will enjoy looking in this safe mirror. Aluminum pie pans, if they are shiny enough, make good mirrors too. Don't forget to hold the baby up in front of a real mirror. Point out the parts of his face and body, and let him touch them. Say "These are Daryl's teeth" when he smiles.

A delightful part of the baby's growing awareness is his sense of humor. He loves to become the center of attention, so when he dances or does something else that he thinks is funny, applaud him. See if he'll continue with an entire group of things that are cute or funny. He'll know what they are, and that he is the one who is making you laugh and applaud. When the baby is showing off, you'll know that he is trying as hard as he can to be a person.

Now, while the baby is trying to establish his self-identity, is a good time to talk about his color. When you talk about the parts and characteristics of his body, you should include skin color. You can also provide the baby with dolls that are black, white, Hispanic or other ethnic types to help make all skin colors normal for him. The baby will not be filled with anxious feelings about his ethnicity as he grows older if you have not either ignored it or overdramatized it.

It's important for you to help the children develop internal control, discipline, direction, and motivation, and it is not too soon to start now. The important thing is that the baby can feel and understand your love and concern for him.

Try to strike a good balance between strictness and permissiveness. Too much in either direction is not good for the baby and may teach him things that you do not want him to learn.

Remember that it is much easier for the baby to learn social techniques if everyone that deals with him at the center treats him in the same way. In this way he knows what to expect; his limits are the same no matter what happens or who is taking care of him at any given moment.

Set up consistent and reasonable limits for him. Let him know that he has the power to affect other adults and children, but that his power is not without limits.

Explanations, such as telling the baby "Now I have to go in the kitchen, Tammy, but I'll soon be back" will help the baby not to be anxious and start acting up.

Preparing the baby for the next activity by telling him what is going to be happening next and giving him time to finish what he is doing will cut down on resistance and conflict.

If you use suggestions instead of commands with the baby, he will be likely to give you less resistance. Suggest for instance, that "Blocks go in the box, Freddy," rather than commanding "Freddy, put those blocks away right now."

One of the most important things that you should teach the baby is to learn how to wait for something. Tell him what is happening and why. For instance, "After I get this cracker for Sibyl, we can play 'Pat-a-cake,' Pete." This way the baby will learn that if he waits a little bit he will often get what he wants. He learns to cooperate and not always expect everything to happen immediately. This is necessary for him to go on to more complicated kinds of learning.

The baby will gradually learn to distinguish between different circumstances if he is handled so that he understands what is expected of him. He'll learn when it's alright to tear, or throw, or run and when it's not. But you have to remember that it takes a long time and a lot of effort on your part to help the baby learn these things. It won't happen overnight. Two important rules that will help you are:

1. Limit your requests of the baby to only those of most importance. If the baby cannot always understand reasons for requests, it will be easier to make fewer requests.
2. When the baby is doing something that you don't want him to, tell him something that he may do, rather than just trying to stop him by saying no.

Now is the time for the baby to begin becoming aware of himself as a person, and his play activities show this. He'll be more choosy about what he wants to do, and you'll find that the articles or tools that you or other adults and children use become of special value. He'll always be on the alert to see how you or others use things, and want to try using them himself.

The baby will start putting all his skills together. For instance, he will use his walking skills to get himself around so that he can better get involved in and learn about his physical world.

It is important for you now to show the baby how to function capably within limits that you set for him without destroying his feeling that he can do things for himself and that he is a capable person.

One important experimentation that goes on now is tapping. The baby will want to get any type of stick and tap it on the floor, or the furniture, or even another person. He's really not using the stick as a tool, but these attempts are the beginning of his use of tools.

Another thing that the baby will start to do is blow. Let him blow out candles or matches for you. He will also like blowing bubbles in a cup. Let him do things with plain water, because he is still too young to blow soap bubbles or bubbles from a commercial mixture. The child might swallow some of the liquid and it might make him ill.

The baby also needs to explore his own muscle power. Let him find out how strong he is by challenging him to see how big a box he can lift, or what size chair he can push, or how many toys he can carry at one time.

Let the baby further his exploratory interests by letting him feel all sorts of different textures. Make a texture poster from various materials, such as flannel, silk, cotton, wool, tree bark, and all the other things that you will be able to think of. Let the baby enjoy running his fingers over all of the items you have put on the poster. Put the poster where all of the children can play with it. Let the baby feel the many things that are soft and hard that you can find in the center. Talk to him about them, and let him contrast how one feels compared to another.

Cut out the side of a plastic milk carton, and plant some seeds in it. Show the baby the new little plants, and teach him to touch them gently. Talk to him about them.

Give the baby a wet sponge, and let him wipe up the floor.

Take the baby on a nature walk in the back yard, and let him fill a box or bucket with rocks, grass and leaves.

Every time you take the baby for a walk, either in the yard or in the neighborhood, encourage him to notice all of the things you see. At first, you will have to point out everything to him, but soon he will be noticing and telling you about things. Encourage this by talking about what he has found, and by being interested in what he sees to tell you about. Remember, it is not how far you walk, but how much both the baby and you enjoy the walk that really matters.

Only walk a few feet for your first walk and only until the baby starts to get tired. Make the walk a little longer each time until the baby can walk for a block or two. Be sure also to leave plenty of time for your walks, so the baby has time to look and explore, without having to be rushed.

115

When the baby is banging his hand or his cup on the table, imitate the rhythm of his banging with another cup, or with your hand. See if he will follow you. Keep playing this game by imitating his other movements and encouraging him to try to imitate you.

Songs with many motions are good to use. "Pat-a-cake" is a very good one. Hold the baby's hands, and sing the song, as you make his hands go through the motions. After you do this several times, try just singing the song, and see if the baby will go through some of the motions by himself. If not, don't be discouraged, just try again later.

Here are some words and motions you can use to teach "Pat-a-cake":

Pat-a-cake, Pat-a-cake, Baker's man,
(clap baby's hands together)
Bake me a cake as fast as you can.
Roll it,
(roll baby's hands)
And pat it,
(pat baby's hands together)
And mark it with . . .
(say initial of baby's first name here)
And put it in the oven for . . . *(say baby's name here)* and me.
(say the last line faster; point baby's hands to him and then you, in time with the words)

You can use records to interest the baby in music, but also try to accompany recorded songs with dances or fingerplays. Be sure that the baby gets involved personally in the action.

Encourage the baby to dance and use his body to the folk tunes that come from his own culture. This way you can help the child learn about his culture.

Make many sound-making toys, such as bells, squeak toys, rattles, and drums available to the baby and try to have a "music" session as often as you can. The children will love it, and learn a lot about their bodies, music, and rhythm.

You'll find that the baby responds to different tempos in music and that he will also enjoy making his own sounds to the music. Imitate the sounds he makes and use them with him.

Vary the lengths of sounds, and make them different degrees of loudness and softness. Let him create sound with his body by clapping, stamping his feet, and yelling or whispering. He can try using his body to make sounds with objects such as banging with a stick on a coffee can drum. Let the child also have the experience of listening to silence.

Sound-producing things can be made from containers filled with sand, beans of different sizes, rice, fresh crackers, colored water, macaroni, salt, popcorn, nuts and bolts, screws, marbles, tacks, jimmies, birdseed, cornmeal, cereal, or pebbles. (For safety, make sure that the toys are securely and tightly sealed. Check every so often on the condition of these toys.)

Give the baby a metal pot with a spoon to clang on it.

A good music maker is a pie plate (aluminum foil) with large bells firmly attached with strong cord or elastic.

Make drums from metal coffee cans with plastic lids firmly attached or from oatmeal boxes. Decorate them attractively, and attach a piece of rope or yarn so they can be worn around the neck.

Attach spools firmly to aluminum pie plates. Give the baby two to clash together as cymbals.

Put pieces of wide elastic with bells firmly attached on the baby's wrists or ankles.

Wooden dowels, cut to about 10 or 12 inches and painted bright colors can be used for drumsticks.

116

The baby may become very fond of a favorite toy or doll, so you should let him have it, especially at nap time, and not tease him about it or with it. The baby needs all of the support he can get get for the loving feeling he shows.

When the baby shows affection for another child, encourage and praise him but don't force him. He may be put off by forcing, and not want to show affection. But if he does pat or kiss another child affectionately, praise him. Say something like "I like the way you gently patted Mary's cheek, Ben."

Sometimes a little accident to another child will show you how affectionate the baby is. If another child hurts his finger, the baby may try to "kiss it and make it better." This is charming and loving behavior, and should always be encouraged.

Let the baby practice doing nice things for the toys he loves. If he has a favorite toy dog or teddy bear, let him give it a drink, or hug it and pat it. You can show him how by patting and hugging it yourself. Don't forget to pat and hug the baby also. He will learn a lot about love and affection from the way you act toward him and the other children.

117

Encourage the baby to do things that he sees other people doing. Let him pretend to talk on the phone, wave "bye-bye" and all the other kinds of actions he sees. You won't find this hard, because the baby will be anxious to try to do what he sees you and others doing. In fact, you may have to be careful to see that he doesn't hurt himself or get into trouble.

Some good ideas for a group of babies to copy are: building small block towers, drawing lines on a large sheet of paper, or eating with a spoon. You can probably think of a lot more of these kinds of things.

The baby may be ready now for a form of "Hide-and-seek." Tell a group of children that you are going to close your eyes while they hide. When you start looking for one of the children, they will probably all call out to you and run to you. You may have to show them what you mean by hiding, and then don't be surprised if they all want to hide in the same place. Show them more than one place to hide.

A good group activity is taking turns on the slide. Let the ones who are new at it or are timid watch while the more experienced children climb up and slide down. Soon they will all be wanting to try.

If the baby is willing, get him involved in group games such as dancing, marching, or singing. Use a lot of motions and facial expressions, and watch the children try to imitate you. Everyone will enjoy these games.

Here are some good motion fingerplays for the group:

I lift my right hand high,
I lift my left hand high,
I clap my hands and then I bow,
And then I walk (march, jump) with you.

Let two or three children sit down, and listen as you sing the following to the tune of "Ten Little Indians":

Where is . . . *(child's name)*, dear little . . . *(child's name)*
(repeat three times)
Way down yonder in the Paw Paw patch.
(Let the child named stand up. If you only
use a group of two or three, you can give
each baby a turn.)

118

As the baby manipulates objects and learns about them, it follows that he will develop a sense of what is "mine" and what is "not mine."

Since toys are desirable objects to the baby, they become part of the baby's growing sense of self. He'll become possessive of them, and want to hide them from others. Now is not the time to expect the baby to share. He may not want to use the toys, but he doesn't want anyone else to have them. The toys are symbols to him of his sense of power; they are *his*. He needs to have them himself, to feel in control of things.

In the day care center, each child may think that all the toys are his. You should try to make certain that each child has some toys or objects that are his private things, for him alone.

Keep group play-time short, and be sure to praise the children for their good behavior. Interest the children in singing, or some other individual activities before such things as toy-grabbing or striking out occur.

Help the baby to learn a sense of responsibility by letting him help put away his own things. Show him that you expect him to take care of his own special things.

You might want to give the baby his own box, with his own name on it. Show him his name, and help him to put his things in it, naming them as you go.

The baby will also enjoy having his own book, and a special "alone" time when he may want to read to himself, or with just you. Try to find time for this with each baby.

Above all, at this stage it is important to realize that the baby has rights to his own things, and he cannot play with other children with very much cooperation. It's important at this time to remember that the baby is still in the developmental stage of playing alone.

119

The baby has many different feelings. He can express fear, jealousy, anxiety, sympathy, anger and other emotions. You can help him to recognize these feelings by naming them for him and talking about them, when he is showing some of these feelings. Let him know that it's alright to feel the way he does, and that sometimes you feel the same way.

Did you know that children who have not been helped to handle their feelings can become very hostile, aggressive and difficult to handle? Or just as bad, a child may hold back his feelings, and this may make him a very quiet and undemanding child, even when he is not being treated fairly. This kind of holding back can lead to the child's failing to learn, and to his having many problems later in his school life.

Let the baby find out that feelings, both good ones and not so good ones, can be talked about and understood. He can also be helped to learn that other people have feelings too.

One of the baby's biggest jobs at this age is to learn to control himself and his feelings, rather than being controlled by you or other people. Try to encourage the baby to express himself, but avoid letting his feelings get out of control. When they show signs of doing so, you should step in, with a firm, no-nonsense voice and look him right in the eye.

If the baby knows you mean it, he'll begin to learn when his feelings are going out of bounds, and will start to have some control over them. But remember, his control is just getting started, and may not yet be linked to his feelings. Here's where it's up to you to talk about these feelings, and help him to understand them.

A good idea is to get the baby involved in why he should do something he's showing unwilling feelings about. For instance, if he's objecting to having his face washed, say to him "You sound like you think I just want to bother you, Le Roy, but let's look in the mirror, and see how much your face needs washing." Let him learn that these things he has to do are for his own good, not for yours or other people's good.

Mirrors are fun, anyway, and you can let the baby look at himself while he shows different emotions. Make happy, sad, etc. faces for him, and let him look at himself when he tries. If you make a "mad" face in the mirror, he'll probably look up at you and laugh. Quickly let him look at himself when he laughs. Talk about all the different feelings he has.

Hang up pictures of people showing different kinds of feelings, and talk about these with the baby. Relate his feelings to those of the people in the pictures. You can do this when you read a book with the baby, too.

Hand puppets will also give you an opportunity to talk about feelings and how they are shown.

Here are a couple of fingerplays about feelings you can use and talk about:

> The gay little cricket
>   Is singing today.
>   He sings at work,
>   Ta dee, ta dum, ta day.

> See the little kitten,
>   As soft as silk,
>   He doesn't like the puppy,
>   But he likes to lap up milk.

> He sputters, "Hiss, hiss, hiss,"
>   When the puppy goes "Grr."
>   And he sings when he's happy,
>   "Purr, purr, purr."

To encourage the baby to play on his own, using his own ideas, be sure to have a large variety of toys and other props that he can get to freely, without having to ask for help.

Have a variety of toys that can be used together, such as blocks, toys, cars and trucks, small dolls and stuffed animals, etc.

Keep a supply of paper and crayons available for him to use, and provide a comfortable place where he can use them.

The center should have an easily reached shelf of books and magazines that he can look at on his own.

He will like to pretend that he is grown-up, doing grown-up things. You can help him do this if you keep a supply of old clothes, especially mommy's and daddy's clothes. He can play store with old grocery cartons, etc. Be sure he has a toy telephone, and other things that grown-ups use.

He should have many dolls, a doll coach, table and chairs, a tea set (unbreakable) and pots and pans. Give him a strong set of plastic knives, forks and spoons. These can be adult picnic size, since he can handle these larger tools better than the tiny toy ones. Just make sure that they are strong, and won't break easily. Examine them, and all of the baby's toys regularly for broken, sharp or jagged edges.

Realize that when you give the baby something new to play with, he will have to examine it thoroughly and see what it's like before he will play with it the way it was meant to be used. Don't rush him.

Did you know that you can make a doll cradle for a small doll from an oatmeal box? Here's how:

HOW TO MAKE A CRADLE:

Materials: *oatmeal carton (round)
*fabric
*glue
*scissors
*paint

Procedure:
1. Cut out about half of the side of the carton; leave the bottom of the box attached.
2. Glue the lid to the open end of the box, making a headboard.
3. Paint the cradle with non-toxic paint.
4. Line the interior by gluing in the fabric.

Now is the time to let the children engage in water and sand play, both indoors and out. Provide them with plenty of spoons, buckets, pots and pans, etc. You might also give them paint brushes, and let them use the water to "paint" the steps, the house, the wall, or anything that water won't harm. Be sure to have some toy cars and trucks for them when they play in the sand. This is very rewarding play for them, and they can be very creative and imaginative with all of these things.

You should, of course, always be with the children to supervise their play, but let them think of things to do themselves. You'll be pleasantly surprised at the amount of imagination and "make-believe" that will come into their play.

121

Parallel play is the stage when the baby plays along with other children, possibly using the same toys, but not really playing with the other children. He sees them as another object to explore along with his other toys. Be careful that he doesn't hurt another child.

Allow the baby many opportunities to play alongside other children. Encourage this by having enough toys for each child to play with several at a time.

In parallel play, you'll see that the children, although playing "alone" or individually, really are very much aware of each other. As one child does something with his toy, another child will try the same thing with his toy. This kind of imitation is a powerful learning force. The children can learn whole "chunks" of behavior in this way from the other children.

It might be a good idea to help the baby begin to use parallel play by first letting him sit close to another child. Let the children explore each other by touching. The baby must find out about another baby the same way he learns about anything. Let them explore each other as long as they both seem to be enjoying it. Guard against injury to either child, though.

When the children are playing well together, in parallel play, reward them by telling them you like how well they are getting along. Be sure to keep the time short when the child play "with" each other. As the children learn not to interfere with each other, you can give them a longer time together.

Children learn quickly when they are left to cope with each other. The other children will show a misbehaving child that they won't put up with him. This is why it's important for you to supervise, but not interfere unless things really get out of hand.

Sandbox play is a good time for parallel play. You might also take the children to neighborhood parks or playgrounds so that they can be around other children they do and do not know well.

A particularly difficult time for the baby is when he first enters the day care center. At this age he is not able to shift his emotions quickly, and a lot of time and patience is required before he will get used to you and the others, and to the routines and activities he'll be involved with at the center. Some misbehavior may occur at first, but perhaps it will be easier for you to cope if you remember that these actions are the baby's way of defending himself in response to the newness of it all.

Try to talk to the baby, and find out what is bothering him if you can. If he knows that he has you to rely on, he will gradually be able to take in and enjoy the new place, people and activities. Realize that at first he may need a lot of soothing support.

Be aware of the child's moods. Sometimes he may be more easily able to get involved with something new, and other times he may not. At these times, let him rely on his old favorite toys or activities.

Remember, one of the first ways that the baby learns to love is through his possessions. You can see him taking care of his toy or doll as though it was his friend. He'll talk to it, give it a ride, try to feed it, and so on. If at all possible, it may be a comfort for him to have it sit with him at the table while he eats. Of course, you should let him nap with it. He needs to feel secure about extending his love.

The baby may be very possessive of his things, his place at the table, and so forth. He'll become very loud in defending what he considers his. It may seem selfish to you, but remember that the baby is trying to develop a clear picture of himself as a separate person.

You and the baby can read books that are old favorites together. This will give him a feeling of security so that he may be better able to try something new later.

If the baby resists doing something new, try not to force him, but let him watch. You may find that as he sees what is happening and begins to feel good about it, he'll gradually join you. This is particularly true of group games like singing and dancing.

If the baby seems to show fear over something new, such as the sound of a siren, he may enjoy a story about firefighters or a toy firetruck. Show him how to make siren noises himself, and let him play with the truck, while making the noise. The other children will probably show him that they are not afraid, and so bolster up his courage. Don't continue if he fails to show interest and still remains frightened.

It will help the baby to be more at home if you hang his picture up along with those of the other children. Point to the picture and say "Who is this?"

Let the baby look at himself in the mirror. He'll be interested to see that he looks like the other children when he does actions that are similar to theirs.

Always write the baby's name on his art work. Ask him where he wants you to write it. You can also ask him where he wants you to hang it up. It is important for him to see his own work admired and looked at by others.

123

When the baby will not cooperate with something you want him to do, try making it more interesting or inviting for him. For instance, if you want him to come to you and he won't, get a favorite toy or doll and show it to him. Ask him to "Come see the teddy bear," and when he does, you can say that teddy wants to help Billy put his jacket on. Involve the toy in the action, so the baby will be interested in doing it also.

Limit the number of times you "order" the baby to do something. Nobody likes to be ordered around. Try to let him make some of his own decisions.

For instance, ask him which foot he wants his shoe on first. These little choices help the baby to learn that he can decide some things on his own.

Remember that baby at this age is trying to become a person in his own right, and he is breaking away from his first earlier dependency. So he will have a "let-me-do-it-myself" attitude, and this usually means that he wants to do what he wants to do, and when he wants to. Now is the time of "No" behavior from the so-called "Terrible Two's." Try to make your needs from him agree with what he wants as often as you can. Be firm, but fair. Let him do what he can do successfully, but stop him, firmly but without getting angry yourself, when enough becomes enough.

Sometimes it's helpful if the baby knows what is expected from him according to routine. Try to do things in a certain order every day, so the baby will get to know what to expect. If he knows, and you don't have to tell him, he may be more cooperative. This gives him a feeling of being effective himself, and of being successful.

Give the baby plenty of time to practice how to do things. He may get frustrated trying to put his sweater on, but he'll get even more frustrated if you put the sweater on for him. He needs to learn this and many other skills, and this takes time. Just remember that it is time well spent. You can make the problem easier if you will only assist him when he has trouble putting on the sweater. Help him by giving it to him right side up, and with the sleeves all turned out right.

When you and the baby are working on learning something new, be sure to keep it short. This way neither you nor the baby will become unhappy with what you are doing.

If the child volunteers to help you, you can return the favor. For instance, if Hank helps you set the table, you can say, "Hank, since you were so nice to help me, I'm going to help you to put your toys away."

124

Now is the time to provide the baby with lots of boxes, old pots and pans, and old clothes, including hats, shoes, scarves, neckties, and other accessories. He needs all of these things, and many more that you'll be able to think of and provide, for him to play with, pretend with, and imagine with.

Things don't have to be exact copies. In fact, the more the baby has to use his imagination, the better it is for him.

You can make a doctor's stethoscope out of an old film can and a piece of string. Attach the string to the can, and let the baby "listen" to your heart.

Make a telephone from two pieces of wood attached with a strip of hose. The baby can talk to you or another child through the hose.

Save old grocery boxes and bags, and let the children play store.

Puppets are particularly good for enlarging a child's imaginative play. He can talk to them, and for them, and about them. Maybe the children would like finger puppets.

HOW TO MAKE A FINGER PUPPET, #1:

Materials: *cardboard
                 *pictures of people and animals

Procedure: 1. Cut the cardboard into a small circle or square.
                 2. Bend cardboard piece into a tube shape and glue or fasten firmly.
                 3. Paste a picture on the cardboard tube.
                 4. Insert finger into tube to make the puppet move.

Encourage the baby to have a tea party with his favorite toys or dolls for company. He will probably get along better with these than with other children, because he is still in the stage of parallel play. However, you might try two children together as long as there are plenty of dishes and toys for all. This is a good way to get the baby started playing *with* another child.

Make sure that the baby has many opportunities to play at being a "mommy" or a "daddy," and let him help sweep or dust, or do other things that grown-ups do.

An old wagon wheel and a chair to sit on will provide the baby with a happy time playing he is driving a car or a truck. Pretend to "fill it up" for him.

In all of the baby's "make-believe" games, be sure to enter into the spirit of things with him. Say "Why, hello, Mr. Smith, how are you today?" and "Yes, thank you, Wilma, you may pour me a cup of tea."

Sometimes it might be fun to reverse your roles. You could pretend to be a child. It's fun to have a tea party this way.

Use action songs and fingerplays that require the use of imaginary actions. "This is the Way We Wash Our Clothes," and "The Wheel on the Bus" are good ones, and you probably know many others.

125

The baby is now at the stage where he must try to sort out his own impulses, and will have great difficulty choosing which ones to follow. Therefore, he'll go to contrary extremes. This is because he is developmentally unable to make a choice, and so must try things out both ways. This will be a difficult time for you, but it will help to remember that the baby is not being contrary on purpose. He is trying to make a wider base of experience for himself, both emotionally and physically.

Try to have a low-key, patient approach. Be tolerant of his zig-zags of behavior, and try to help him learn smoother, easier ways to cope with his impulses.

Sometimes if the baby seems stubborn or frightened, you and he can talk about and play out what seems to be bothering him. For instance, if he doesn't want to take a nap, you can "make-believe" that he and you are putting the dolly to bed for a nap. He may pretend that the dolly doesn't want to go to sleep, and then he and you can "talk" to the dolly. After he has talked about and pretends that another has his problem, he may then be ready to take his nap. He will have experienced both sides of a question, and so can go on from there.

The baby has contrary impulses of wanting to be on his own, yet needing you to help him solve problems for him. He can't have both at once, and so he has to learn to give a little both ways. Your job is to help him gain this kind of control.

Many of the day's rough spots will come over the routine events, such as naptime, getting dressed, and so forth. It's best if you adopt a calm but firm attitude that routines are a matter of course and not open to question.

It's very important to find ways to set reasonable limits for the baby, without discouraging him from exploring and learning about his world. If the baby needs to be stopped from what he is doing, substitute another activity that will distract him from what you don't want him to do, or perhaps a few simple directions, spoken in a firm but pleasant tone, will stop the baby. If these both fail, quietly pick up the baby and take him away from where he is and put him where he should be.

Always praise the baby with attention and applause when the child's behavior is what is should be. Don't reward behavior that is not wanted. Your shouting and punishing the child may result in his thinking that he can get more attention from you when he misbehaves. Some children want attention so badly that they will misbehave on purpose.

The "tantrum" or "no" behavior may last for quite some time, but since this is part of the baby's normal development it is nothing to worry about. The baby will go on for days with no problems, and then go back to his "no" behavior. Try to think that the baby's "ups" must be balanced by his "downs." They are necessary for his total developmental progress. We are raising our children to live in a complicated and demanding society, and this kind of behavior seems to be necessary so that the children will develop the qualities they need to cope with society today.

126

You'll find that the baby is now at the "snatch and grab" stage. And in keeping with his contrary behavior, he will sometimes be shy and at other times aggressive. He is still in the parallel play stage, but may be able to start doing things with other children.

Be sure to reward the child when he does play well with or near another child. Say something like "I like to watch you and Debby playing tea party so nicely, Marvin."

Children can start playing together very easily when they play "house" or play in the sandbox, or have fun with water play. Just be sure to have plenty of equipment and supplies for all to use. Don't forget though, you must be there with them all of the time.

Maybe the baby just wants to stand and look at the other children play. Don't force him into the group, but encourage him to watch. Let him join in when he is ready.

Try to stay out of squabbles that arise as long as the children seem to be able to deal with it themselves. Be ready to step in, if there is any danger of one child injuring another. You should be there, but in the background, letting the children handle their own play situations.

Be careful that you don't over-protect the children. If you jump in at the slightest cry or fall, you'll be telling the children that there is something to be afraid of. They have to experience and survive many minor disasters to learn that the world is not too dangerous for them to venture into.

Conflict among the children must be handled through a trial and error process. Sometimes you must separate the children; sometimes they can handle it themselves. Sometimes if you remove whatever they are fighting over, that will do the trick; sometimes you may have to isolate one child until he can control himself again; sometimes you can give the children something new and interesting to do; sometimes you can "talk" the problem out with the children. Keep in mind that you should remain calm, yet firm; consistent, yet fair.

The baby's first group play should be short, simple and supervised. Two to three children are as large a group as each baby can handle at first. Expect them to be very possessive about favorite toys. The child will let someone else play with them only for the moment. That's one reason why you should give them many toys to choose from. Remember, it takes years to learn to take turns and to share.

Other activities that lend themselves to helping the children learn to play together are blowing bubbles, finger painting, swings, blocks, tricycles, and simple games like "Ring-Around-The-Rosy."

You'll find that the baby loves to play with his fingers and toes. You can help him learn if you'll name or count his fingers and toes. Name, touch, and talk about his other body parts also.

Here's some simple rhymes you can use:

Good morning, Mr. Thumb-O.
How do you feel today?
Jump around and take a bow,
Then run, run, run away.
(Continue this rhyme with each finger and toe—you can say "Good morning, Finger One-O, etc.)

Here are baby's eyes,
Here is baby's nose,
Touch the part that sees,
Touch the part that blows.

Up-up-up,
My baby goes,
Reach way up,
And touch my nose.

Down-down-down,
My baby goes.
Reach way down,
And touch your toes.

Other finger and toe games that you probably already know are "Thumbkin," "Pat-a-cake," and "This Little Piggy Went to Market." Both you and the baby will have a wonderful time with these games, but the important part is that the baby is learning the names of things, even if he can't say them yet.

Let the baby watch a hand puppet or a finger puppet. Make it dance and sing. The sillier the puppet looks and acts, the more the baby will like it.

HOW TO MAKE A FINGER PUPPET, #2:

Materials:
*finger from an old glove
*embroidery thread or felt
*bottle top that fits down over your finger
*glue
*needle

Procedure:
1. Sew or glue eyes, nose, mouth, and hair to bottle top.
2. Attach bottle top head to the finger of the glove.

Put the baby's hand on your nose, mouth or eyes, and name them in a clear, loud voice. Then touch the baby's nose, etc. and say the name again. If you have a group of children together, you can do this in turns with each, while the others watch. Make a surprise game of whose turn is next. They will all be delighted and fascinated.

Play rattle games with the baby. Hold out a bright colored one for him to grab, first with one hand and then with the other. Try giving it to him from different positions and different heights.

To encourage the baby to play with his feet, let him frequently play with his shoes and socks off. Make a "funny" foot sock for him.

HOW TO MAKE A "FUNNY" FOOT SOCK:

Materials:
*old bright-colored baby socks
*felt and yarn scraps
*scissors
*needle and thread

Procedure:
1. Cut eyes, nose, etc., from felt.
2. Sew face on the socks, with the top of the head and eyes at the toe end.
3. Sew on yarn for hair.

The baby must learn that you will respond to his babbling "baby talk" with sounds and words of your own. This teaches the baby that sound and speech are important.

Start a game with the baby: look into his eyes, make a sound and then let him do it. You could do it the other way around also; you imitate the sounds you hear the baby making. Pretty soon you won't know if he is imitating you or you are imitating him.

After you and he have been imitating each other for a while, start to change your sounds so that they sound like the beginning of a word. For instance, if the baby says, "Ba, ba, ba," you can say these sounds as if you were going to say "baby." Perhaps after a while you can say the whole word. Always give the baby a chance to imitate you.

One thing that is very important for the baby, in fact necessary, is for you to talk to him whenever he is awake. It doesn't matter if he cannot understand you. This will help the baby to learn patterns of language, and how important language really is.

It is also important for you to sing to him and rock him at the same time. The rocking motion will help the baby enjoy the rhythm. Rhythm plus singing patterns are also important for the baby to learn so that he will later be able to speak. Remember to do both of these important things for the baby while you are giving him routine care all during the day.

Give the baby as many experiences with his senses as possible. Give him many different things to feel, to see, to hear, to touch, and to taste.

If you can get hold of a tape recorder, try taping sounds the baby makes. Play it back to the baby. The sound of his own voice will encourage the baby to keep on talking.

When you "talk" to the baby, sometimes whisper, and sometimes make your voice louder. Speak in high and low tones, laugh and giggle, speak slowly and quickly. If the baby "talks" to you, wait until his sentence is over, and then talk to him some more, imitating his sounds or just talking naturally. The more you talk, the more the baby will "talk."

Always call the baby by name when you are talking to him. Wait until he looks at you before you go on talking. For instance, say "Dickie, here's a cracker," or "Come on, Milly, it's time for lunch." Don't forget to always name all the things that you use and do with the baby all day long.

If you always use the baby's name when you talk to him, he will soon begin to know that it is his own "special" word, and look toward you when you say it. He may also respond by babbling to you.

It's a good idea to always name the objects that the baby is especially interested in, such as his bottle. If he always sees a bottle when he hears you say "bottle," he'll soon learn that the word you are saying is the name for it. This is a big step forward for the baby, as he begins to understand that words name things.

The baby may look at you when you say his name, or at the door when it slams. These actions tell you that the baby understands more than he can talk about. So even if he can't tell you, you can be sure that the baby is always learning.

When you and the baby are doing anything together, always put your actions into words. Say what you are doing with the baby as you are doing it, for example, "Now let's put your hat on, Mike."

The baby will be helped to understand speech if you use motions, and tell him what they mean. Name the motions he makes too. For instance, if he holds up his arms to be picked up, say "Uh-oh, Mark wants to be picked up."

Give the baby toys that can be easily named, such as a cup, a doll, etc., and name them for him as you give them to him.

Talk about sounds you and the baby hear during the day. Give the sounds names. Say something like, "Oh, Janie, there goes the telephone ringing." Make other sounds yourself, such as tapping or drumming, and name them for the baby.

Encourage the baby to crawl, since this action has an indirect affect on speech. It helps to mature certain nervous system functions which are necessary for the baby to speak. Crawling also helps the baby to gain many more experiences by widening his world. So turn the baby loose and let him explore.

Play word games with the baby. For instance, wave "goodby," and let the baby wave back to you. Do this with other motions so he can both see the action and hear what it is called.

When you sing rhymes and songs, or do fingerplays with the baby, always use the baby's own name instead of just saying "baby."

It's your job to say the names of all the people and objects that the baby comes in contact with. Say them and the baby's own name over and over for him. Wrap him in a constant blanket of words and sentences. This is one of the most important things you can do.

As you get to know the baby better and better, you will almost always know what he's trying to say. When he does say a real word, repeat it and show him, if possible, the object or person he has just correctly named.

Respond to the baby whenever you are holding or tending him by repeating the sounds he is making. Pat his stomach, and move your head close enough so that he can see and hear you smiling and "talking" to him.

Hold the baby in front of a mirror and let him talk to himself. You can even let him hold an unbreakable one. He'll gabble to the baby in the mirror and have a delightful time.

While you are talking to the baby, you'll find that he will respond by babbling back to you and smiling. This is his way of asking you to keep on talking. Keep him happy and interested in "talking" by letting him see you always smiling and talking to him and to other people.

Encourage the baby to listen for all the various sounds he can hear during the day. Name them for him. Remember that as you teach the baby to listen for sounds, you are also teaching him how to listen. This is very important for the development of his speech.

A good "sound" game to play with the baby is to get several plastic jars or bottles of different sizes. Fill them to various levels and then, while the baby watches and listens, tap them with a spoon so he can hear the different sounds they make. He'll want to try it too. You can let him, but stay right there with him. He shouldn't be left on his own with bottles of water.

Another way to help the baby listen is to play a hiding game. Hide in back of something and call the baby softly by name. When he starts to look for you, pop out so he can see you.

Help the baby to understand that sounds tell us things. The ringing of the bell means the telephone, for instance, or the crackling sound of the wrapping means a cookie.

The baby also learns meaning from the way your voice sounds. Loud may mean anger, and soft and cooing may mean love. Experiment with the baby by using several different levels and tones of voice. See how he reacts.

Give the baby many toys that make squeaks and other noises. Pots and pans are also fun and the baby can make wonderful sounds with them. This may not be so easy on your ears, but remember, the baby needs noisy play to help him learn about sounds.

A squeaking picture book is also a good way for the baby to learn about sound. You can find instructions for making one in *Activity #72.*

The baby loves to imitate you, so hold him in your lap and make sounds that are the sounds of speech. Use "da," "ma," "fa," "ba," etc. These are the ones easiest for him to make. When he correctly imitates you, show him you are proud of him. Smile and hug him, so he knows you think it's fun. Don't just use any of the sounds he makes—use only the ones that you know can be used in words.

Don't forget to point out to the baby the noises that animals and other things make. Tell him that the kitty goes "meow," the cow goes "moo," and so on. This helps to build memory patterns that are meaningful for speech.

131

Now the baby's language or speech is starting to come. He will use words or sounds of one or two syllables, while naming objects or people familiar to him. His first words will probably be "mama" or "dada," and they will soon be followed by "doggie," "kitty," and so forth.

At first, the baby will use single words instead of a whole sentence to tell you something. He may say "car" or "hat" when he really means "I want a car" or "Put my hat on." You will know by his motions and the tone of his voice what he means.

The baby will say many words wrong, and it will sound cute to you. For instance, he may say "twuck," for "truck." You'll be tempted to say the word the way he says it. But after all, you are trying to teach the baby the right way to say things, and he might never hear it the right way if you don't say it correctly. Remember, "example is the best teacher." Set a good example for the baby.

As the baby learns new words, give him as many chances as you can to use them. For instance, if the baby can say "car," give him toy cars to play with. Ask him what they are every once in a while. Also be sure that he has a chance to say his new words for the person who brings him and picks him up, and for others in the center. Show the child you're proud of him.

If possible, try to get some photos of the mothers and fathers of the babies in the center. Mount the pictures low on the wall and cover them with plastic. Now the babies can name their own "people" as they look and point to the pictures. Pictures of the babies themselves can also be mounted in the same way. The baby will look at his own picture and begin to call it by name.

Talk to the baby about things that you and he are doing by using complete sentences. He will not be able to do this yet, but he needs to hear it from you. Say "Now, Barry, we are washing your hands," for example. Remember to always include the baby's name in the sentence.

Play telephone games with the baby. Ring a bell, and let him answer you on his toy phone. Talk to him and try to get him to answer and talk to you.

Play records for the baby where words to songs, etc., are the ones he can understand. Sing and encourage the baby to sing along with you.

You can begin to sing nursery rhymes with the baby, and to do fingerplays with him. Keep them simple and familiar. The baby will like to do the same ones many times over.

Here's some the baby will like:

> Knock at the door,
> Peep in—
> Lift the latch,
> Walk in.
>
> The great big train
> Goes up the track.
> It says, "Toot, toot,"
> And then it goes back.
>
> Here is a box,
> And here is the top.
> Lift the lid,
> Out Jack *(or use baby's name)* will pop.

Remember that babies love to be sung to. It won't matter to them how you sound. They also won't know or care if you know all the words of a song. Make up your own. In fact, you can make up your own songs about what you and the baby are doing. This will interest the baby and keep him listening to you.

Cut out the pictures of several objects that the baby is familiar with. Mount them on a large piece of cardboard or on the wall. Cover them with clear plastic and play a game with the baby. Name the object and see if the baby can point to it. Soon he will be able to say some of the names as you point to the objects.

Put some toys in a box and ask the baby to hand you the one you name. See if he will also say the name. Make a fuss over him when he is right. Show him you are proud of him.

Take the baby for a short walk outdoors. Here you can name many things for him that he doesn't see in the house. Point out and name a bird, a leaf, a bus, and all the other things that you and the baby will see. Use simple names for things, but make sure they are the right names.

Make a scrapbook for the baby that has large, simple pictures of things that the baby is familiar with. The baby can sit on your lap while you show him the pictures and name them for him.

The baby will enjoy looking at all large picture books and magazines. Point to the things in the pictures when you and he are reading together. Say "Look, Eric, here is a tree, and this is a house," etc. He'll soon be able to point to the right picture when you name it, and before long he'll be saying the names himself. Be sure he knows you are proud of his progress.

The baby should also have time to sit by himself and look at picture books. Use very sturdy books. His first book could be made of cloth. Let him look at the books any way he wants to. This will keep him interested and if you listen, you'll hear him start to name some of the pictures he sees.

Point out familiar pictures of objects wherever they appear. You can find them on package or jar wrappers, on the cereal box, and on many everyday items you use with the baby.

The baby may talk to himself sometimes about what he is doing. He will probably use simple, small words. Don't make fun of him when he does this. He needs to do this to get experience with talking and understanding about things.

The important thing about talking to the baby is to keep it up. Almost any remarks, even if the baby cannot understand them, are better than silence. But don't expect the baby to be interested in something just because you are.

Notice what the baby is interested in and talk to him about that. If he's not interested, he won't be listening.

Something that may happen is that the baby will forget. He may be able to tell you the name of a toy one time, and then not be able to the next time. This is a perfectly natural development. Just begin to teach him again. You'll find that this pattern may repeat itself several times before the idea takes permanent hold in the baby's mind.

Always remember that the baby doesn't learn language through direct teaching or imitation of words that you say. He may learn a few words this way, but he'll learn most from hearing you talk about the actions you do and naming them for him.

If you always talk to the baby in a natural way, he'll be able to hear and learn the natural patterns of speech. This is why you should use short but complete sentences and no baby talk when you are talking to the baby. If the baby learns baby talk from you, then he'll have to unlearn it in order to speak well.

Perhaps the baby will invent words of his own to name some object or action. He might, for instance, call cereal "skippies." You can use his word when you are talking about his cereal. This helps to build a bridge of meaning between his language and the real word, since he'll hear you using the word "cereal" when you are talking about it to the other children. Don't invent your own baby talk, though.

Since the baby learns to use and understand language by the association between words and actions, you should always name and describe the actions that you are both doing. If you say, "Hold out your hand," to the baby when nothing else is happening, he won't understand. But if you pick up his mitten and show it to him as you say, "Hold out your hand, Gilbert, so we can put your mittens on," the baby will understand. The more he understands, the more he will try to use words to make you understand him.

When you are using an object with the baby, use its name several times to reinforce it. For instance, you can say something like, "Kim, do you want a cookie? Look at this nice cookie. I bet you'll like this nice round cookie." This is not baby talk, although it may sound like baby talk to you. Make sure to do the same when you are talking about and naming activities for him.

The baby can now speak a few words. You'll notice that he babbles and jabbers in a way that almost sounds like real speech. His babbling is imitating the rhythm and flow of real speech, and is part of the way the baby learns speech patterns. He is bridging the gap between the few words he does know how to say and the continous flow of sound when an adult speaks. This type of speaking is called "Jargon." The baby sometimes will do it so well that you'll get the feeling you can almost understand what he is saying.

Build sentences for the baby, using words that he can say. If he can say cup, for instance, answer him by saying, "Yes, this is your cup, Doug. Do you want some milk from your cup?" As you are talking, match your actions to what you are saying. This helps the baby to put the ideas of words and actions together for himself.

Remember to always use simple sentences, but talk to the baby. Talk about what you are doing, name things for him, respond to his attempts to speak. You can make the baby's whole day a workshop for learning to speak.

The baby is beginning to know and name familiar objects and activities because you have helped him by always using their names in sentences when you talked to the baby. You have done good work. Keep it up, and the baby will keep on learning to say more and more words. It is believed that much of the desire to use language and learn to read starts in the baby's earliest years.

Help the baby to learn the names of common objects he's familiar with by naming things for him, and asking him to point to them. For instance, you might try showing him a cup and a block. Pick up one of the objects and ask him to name it. Praise him if he names it correctly. If he is wrong, say "No, Darren, that is not the cup." Then pick up the cup and say, "See, this is the cup."

You can also try asking the baby to point to an object that you name. When he does, then you can ask him its name. Be careful that you don't frustrate the baby. You can always stop and try again later.

Sometimes you'll find that the baby's words have a very general meaning. He'll call all of the stuffed animals or the ones he sees in pictures "doggie." You can try to help him understand that they are all animals, but they are not all "doggies." Whenever you are talking to him about animals, you can say something like, "This animal is a horse, Jessie, and this animal is a pig." If you keep doing this, the baby will gradually learn that each animal is just that, but that it has its own name, too.

On the other side of the coin, you should also help the baby to learn that many things of different sizes and colors are still called by the same name. For instance, you can give the baby a group of cups of different sizes, shapes and colors. Tell him as you pick each one up that it is a cup. Then let him point to and name them.

Help the baby to learn names of objects and who owns them by asking the child to do small jobs for you. You could say, "Here, Debra, take this spoon to Mrs. Smith. It is her spoon," or "Can you find me your new red hat, Kevin?" Praise him when he does what you have asked. Above all, don't let the baby become discouraged or feel that he has failed. If he doesn't seem to be able to understand, stop and try another time.

Help the baby to learn some other ideas about things by using words that describe objects. Tell him and show him something that is hard, or soft, or fuzzy, or smooth, etc. You can also tell and show him about size (large, small, wide, narrow, etc.) or about colors. He won't be able to say all of these things yet, but he'll learn gradually if you keep on using these words that describe things.

If you are giving the baby several items, such as cookies, you can count them as you give them to him. See if he'll try to say the names after you. You can't expect him to actually learn to count, but this is adding "number" words to his speech. This is important for arithmetic development later on. Here are some other counting activities:

Counting fingers and toes
Counting blocks and toys as you use them
Learning "How old are you?"
Counting pictures or real objects
Counting cars, buses, and trucks as they go by

Show the baby real objects and pictures of objects. See if he can name them and match them up.

When you see things pictured in a book, ask the baby what it does. For instance, when you see a picture of a cup, pretend that you are drinking from a cup. Pretty soon the baby will be doing the same when he sees a picture of a cup.

Glue pictures of objects on the outside of two large paper grocery bags. Give the baby the two real objects, and let him sort these into the right bag by matching it with the picture. Pictures of fruit are particularly good here, since the baby can touch, taste and smell the fruit that he is to match with the picture.

Help the baby to sort real objects by placing some in front of him. You could try, for instance, blocks and toy cars. Then you can ask him to put all the cars in a certain place. Don't be surprised if he can't do it. Show him what you mean. Say "We'll put the green cars here, Susan, and the red blocks over here." Talk about the objects and your actions as you do it. Describe them. Let the baby try if he wants to, but if he doesn't, just let him play with the two sets of objects in his own way.

The baby can try matching pictures. Place two pictures in front of him. Then hold a picture that matches one of them in your hand. Ask him to find the picture that matches it.

The baby can start color matching with two different colors. Put a piece of paper of each color in front of him and give him a piece of paper the same color as one of them. See if he can place the one he has next to the one that matches. Be sure to use very different colors, such as red and blue, or yellow and green.

IMPORTANT: Always use only two choices for beginning sorting games.

The important thing in helping the baby learn to speak is using words and sentences with him while having a pleasant experience. One of the best ways to do this is to hold the baby on your lap and look at books. While you read to him, he turns the pages. The baby's closeness to you and the sound of your voice in this happy situation will make him feel secure, so that he will try talking and pointing out things.

When you are reading or singing, always make the baby the center of the activity. Look at him, point things out to him, and act especially pleased when he tries to sing or name things for you.

As you are reading a story to the baby, ask him things about it. You could ask, for example, "What is the little girl doing, Georgie?" or "Juan, does the kitty have a name?"

If the baby seems to have trouble naming pictures in the book, try to find real items that are the same as the pictured item. Then you can ask the baby to put the apple with the picture of the apple, for instance. Now the baby has more than one way to learn. He can see, feel, smell, and sometimes even hear the real objects from the page of the book. It may take him a while to know that the picture only represents the real thing.

Remember as you look at books with the baby, you are not in any way trying to teach him to read. You only want to make him aware of reading and reading materials. Reading with him joins his interest in what you do with your attention to him and the book.

As you look at the books you plan to read to the baby, find pictures that come up quite often in the same book. This will help the baby become familiar with and to recognize the same picture each time. Also try to make sure that the book has pictures of things you know the baby is familiar with. A gradual introduction to new and unfamiliar pictures may be started as the baby becomes more and more familiar with his first books.

Make sure that the baby has plenty of magazines and mail order catalogs to use and look at the way he wants to. Let him do what he wants to do with them. If he doesn't completely wreck the one he's looking at, give it to him again the next time. He'll enjoy this because now he is familiar with it, and he can look for details that he missed before.

Use your imagination and make a textured picture book for the baby.

HOW TO MAKE A CLOTH PICTURE BOOK:

Materials: *6″ to 8″ squares of fabric with good body, such as felt, heavy knits, corduroy, etc.
*cut-outs of familiar animals, flowers, and other shapes
*needle and thread
*pinking shears
*glue

Procedure: 1. Trim the edges of the fabric with pinking shears.
2. Sew fabric squares together on one side to form pages of the book, using strong thread. Sew back and forth several times.
3. On each page sew or glue a picture cut-out. Use contrasting colors for cut-out and page.
4. Add details to pictures, such as cotton ball tail, yarn for hair, etc. Use your imagination here. You can even put "squeaks" in some of them.

A variation of this book could be made by following these directions to make the pages, and then sewing a working zipper on one page, working buttons or snaps on another page, or perhaps a mitten on another page that the baby could put his hand in. Use your imagination here too, and make a "do-it-yourself" book for the baby.

136

The baby needs many fingerplays and songs to learn how to coordinate his body actions and voice. This is important in language learning. How many times do we find that we communicate with gestures in addition to speech? These activities also help the baby to learn the names of all the actions we do every day. There are many good songs and fingerplays that you can use. Try "The Wheels on the Bus," "Here We Go 'Round the Mulberry Bush," or "Ring-Around-A-Rosie."

These kinds of games are also good because they encourage group play. If some of the babies don't want to take part, don't force them. They will soon join in on their own, when they see how much fun everyone is having. It is important for the children to have group experience and interplay so that they can begin to try out their language on each other.

Children in day care or other school settings use more language with each other than they do with their teachers. So it's important that they get the chance to talk and interact with each other as soon as they can.

Here are some more good action verses for you to try with the children:

This is the way the baby does,
Clap . . . Clap . . . Clap . . . Clap;
This is the way the baby does,
Peek-a-boo, I see you;
This is the way the baby does,
Creep . . . Creep . . . Creep . . . Creep;
This is the way the baby does,
Sleep . . . Sleep . . . Sleep . . . Sleep.

Sailing boat, sailing boat,
Go so slow.
Sailing boat, sailing boat,
Go so fast.

The children should have experiences hearing loud and soft tones, fast and slow music, and so on. The children will have fun learning what these words mean and trying to sing or talk in these different ways.

Encourage the children to make sounds with their bodies. They can clap, jump, stamp, and so on. They can also make sounds with sticks or drums to bang, bells and triangles to ring, etc. Let them march or dance to music, too.

Here's a good verse for making different sounds and motions:

Here's a ball for baby, big, soft and round.
Here is baby's hammer; oh, how he can pound.
Here is baby's music, clapping, clapping so.
Here are baby's soldiers, standing in a row.

Here is baby's trumpet, too-too, too-too, too-too,
Here's the way the baby plays at peek-a-boo.
Here's the big umbrella to keep the baby dry.
Here is baby's cradle, rock a baby bye.

The baby will probably now be very interested in his body parts, as a part of his growing sense of awareness. You and he can sit and talk together about your body parts. You can touch his nose, for example, and say, "Here is Robert's nose," and then touch your nose and say "And this is my nose." Do this with your other body parts. Make it like a game. Let the baby touch your nose, mouth, etc. and then his own. See if he can name any of them as you say them to him. Then ask him to show you his ear, for instance. Go on with this until the baby gets tired. He'll think it's fun, however, and it may be quite a while before he tires of this game.

It's fun to try the above games while both of you are looking in the mirror. Then the baby will have three places to point out and name an ear, an eye, or whatever.

During your daily activities together you should always say the names of body parts you are using. Say, "Come on, Kim, let's wash your hands," or "Put the cookie in your mouth, Kara." This will teach and reinforce names and uses of body parts for the baby.

Sit down with the baby and a large sheet of paper and draw pictures of people. As you put in the body parts, say "Here's the man's hair, Wilma," or "What parts am I drawing now, Sonya?" If you ask the baby such a question, he may just point to his own body part. This is fine, but keep on saying the body parts, and soon he will be able to both point to and name the part.

Another thing you can help the baby to learn is what the body parts do. He'll learn about this more quickly if you use actions along with your words. Place your hands over his eyes so that he cannot see. Then ask him to make sure he can't see. Help him to put his hands over his eyes. Do this with other body parts, such as ears, etc. Talk to him about using his feet and legs to run, and so forth. Don't forget to also include the senses, such as smelling or tasting when you are talking about his body. Let him smell, taste things, for instance, and talk about the way they smell, taste, etc.

Give the baby a large doll to play with, and you'll find that he'll begin to play all these games with the doll, just as you did with him. Use fingerplays about body parts with the baby. Here are a couple of verses you can use:

Head and shoulders, knees and toes,
Head and shoulders, knees and toes,
Head and shoulders, knees and toes,
We'll all jump down together.
(Then start with toes and work back up again; use motions and sing this to the tune "Here We Go 'Round the Mulberry Bush.")

I have ten little fingers,
And ten little toes,
Two little arms,
And one little nose,
One little mouth,
And two little ears,
Two little eyes,
For smiles and tears,
One little head,
And two little feet,
One little chin,
And that's *(child's name)* complete.

138

Be sure to start the baby with only one step directions. If you ask him to go get his shoes and put them under his cot, you'll find that he can only do the first part. He may bring you the shoes, but he won't remember what to do with them.

You'll make it easier for the baby if you make gestures as you ask him things. He'll understand better if you point to cookies and then to your mouth as you ask him to give you a cookie.

It's important to reward the baby with a smile or a hug to show him how pleased you are that he was able to do as you asked. This is the best kind of reward for him, maybe even better than a piece of candy or a new toy.

Practice giving the baby directions. Make a game of it for the baby, and let him enjoy doing what you request for as long as he is interested. The baby will be anxious to try to do as you ask because he likes you and looks up to you. Actually, he is engaged in one of life's first business deals. He exchanges doing what you ask for your love and approval.

Begin with easy directions that the baby can do and wants to do. Show him how to wave "Bye-bye," how to play "Peek-a-boo," and so forth. He needs to have fun while learning to follow directions.

Let the baby do things with a favorite toy or doll. See if he can make it walk, sit, or lie down, etc. Encourage him to give these kinds of directions to the doll, and then to make it do them. Or you can give directions so the baby and doll can follow them. He'll make the doll do it, and then do it himself, and have lots of fun while he's at it. He'll also learn the words for these directions, and other actions. Words, you see, are learned through actions.

You can try a simple game of "Simon Says," with the baby. Just make a simple motion, such as bowing, and say "Simon says to bow." Do it again while the baby does it with you. He may even be able to make some motions and name them for you to follow.

Use songs and fingerplays that have directions in them for the baby to follow. Here's a good one:

Two little hands go clap, clap, clap,
Two little feet go tap, tap, tap,
Two little arms reach high in the air,
One little person jumps up from his chair,
Two little fists go thump, thump, thump,
Two little feet go jump, jump, jump,
One little person turns slowly around,
Folds his arms and sits quietly down.
(If this seems too long, just use the first two or four lines.)

The baby can say a large number of names for things now. He will proudly point to and name many objects. This gives him a feeling of control over these things, which is what he needs to help him go on learning.

Now through his naming, the baby is beginning to recognize that the world may be divided up into various kinds of things, actions, etc. Encourage this in the baby by always naming all of the things you use, do, and so forth. Ask him to name things, too, and you'll find he's learning more and more.

Actions and the thoughts that the baby has about them will come before the baby can say the words. This is why you need to involve the baby in a lot of actions that you name for him. Make sure the actions include shapes, sizes and colors, textures, and so forth.

It's going to be harder for the baby to understand and use pronouns. These words are confusing. You can begin to use the words "you," "your," etc. When talking to the baby, say "Here's a cookie for you," or "This red hat goes on your head," instead of using the baby's own name as you've been doing. Use a lot of other pronouns, too. Say "He is running to her," or "I am going to sit down," instead of using actual names. Remember, though, that using the baby's own name occasionally won't hurt and will make the baby feel good.

One way to help the baby learn about pronouns and other parts of speech is to hang pictures of the children where they can all see them. They'll stay cleaner if you cover them with clear plastic. You'll find that looking at these pictures will provide many chances for the children to try using pronouns. You and the children can talk about what is happening in the pictures, saying things like, "Look at your pretty dress," and "I can see both you and me in this picture." Use motions also as you talk to the children, so they'll connect the words and the actions.

The words listed below are all words that can become part of the baby's speech. Remember, children learn new words quickly when you can show what they mean. Use these words and others that you'll be able to think of. Suggestions about the ways you can show the baby the meanings are listed below:

Hot: Hot water or milk, your hot coffee, cocoa.
Cold: Juice or milk, ice and snow, your hands when it's cold.
Slow or Fast: Body actions, music and rhythm, making toy cars go.
Stop or Go: Use the same ideas as in slow or fast.
Over or Under: Body parts, boxes, blocks, pictures, toys, tables, chairs.
Full or Empty: A cup (before and after drinking from it), the cookie box.
Large or Small: Blocks, boxes, dolls, shapes, people (such as you and the baby).
Open or Shut: Boxes, books, doors, hands.
Boy or Girl: Pictures, photographs, the children themselves.
Round or Square: Shapes, boxes and balls, objects in the room, pictures.
Down or Up: Body actions, where things are kept, play "Ring-Around-the-Rosie."
Quiet or Loud: Music and singing, voices inside and voices outside, walking, speaking.

The baby's ability to learn and use language is growing rapidly now. It's up to you to continue to provide many opportunities for him to correctly learn and use language. Talk to him in a normal way—the way you would talk to anyone. Talk to him about the many things around you, and the activities that you and he are doing. This will not only help to improve his language, but it will also give his curiousity a push, and make him observe what is going on around him. This is important for language development.

Listen to what the baby has to say about things. The baby needs to know that when he talks to people they are ready to listen and respond. This is very important. The baby must be encouraged, not discouraged to talk. If he thinks that no one cares or is interested in what he says, he may soon give up trying to talk and learn new words.

On the other hand, don't be too insistent on the baby learning and using new words. Be sure he wants to learn them. Most children do, but if the baby is having trouble with his language use, you may hopelessly frustrate him. If the baby should stop speaking or seems very slow learning words, it may be because there is too much pressure on him to speak. Remember too that sometimes a child's voice equipment may not be matured enough to produce certain sounds in speech. The age at which a child starts to talk and the amount of talking varies with every child.

Another thing that will slow the baby down is when he hears one language at home and another at the center. It will probably take him a little longer to learn, but don't worry, he'll catch up.

Reading to the baby is always very important, but make sure that the baby is enjoying the story even if he doesn't understand every word. From your reading to the baby, he can learn how to say things and what to call things. He'll also be improving his skills of listening and remembering. You can ask the baby some questions as you're reading to find out if he understands and if he is interested.

The baby may want you to read certain stories or books over and over again. He will begin to say some of the words with you. This is a first step toward reading. It may get boring for you to read a story over and over again, but stop reading it only when the child gets bored with it, not when you do.

Back the baby up by expanding his sentences, like this:

The baby says:	*The caregiver says:*
"Ball	"Yes, that's a ball."
"Cookie?"	"Do you want a cookie?"
"Hot"	"Yes, the stove is hot!"

A toy that will provide the children with much practice in talking and listening is a walkie talkie. Here's how to make one:

HOW TO MAKE A WALKIE TALKIE:

Materials:
*two 10-15 oz. tin cans
*one or two yard piece of string
*plastic tape

Procedure:
1. Remove tops from cans and wash thoroughly. Make sure the edges are very smooth and will not cut, then cover with plastic tape.
2. Punch a hole in the bottom of each can. Be sure the jagged edge of the hole is inside the can. Cover it with plastic tape.
3. Insert string inside each of the cans, through the hole, from outside to inside.
4. Knot the string inside each of the cans. Make sure it is secure.
5. Have the baby talk into the can while you listen, and then let him listen while you talk.

141

Now that the baby has made the very important discovery that everything, everybody, and every action has a name, he'll always be asking you, "What's that?" You'll get tired of hearing it, but don't get tired of giving him the answer.

When you are sure that the baby knows the name of several objects, collect them and put them in front of him. See if he can pick out the right one when you name it, then let him try naming the various articles as he points to them. This may take a lot of practice before he gets good at it.

Matching is a part of learning the names of things. Some things are different, yet they have the same name. Help the baby learn this by grouping things together. Tell him that his doll, his teddy bear, his truck are all called toys, for instance. You can also place several different types of cups in front of him, and show and tell him that each one is a cup. Show him that each cup can do what every cup does. You can find lots of articles to help the baby learn this.

Cut out pictures that match, and paste them on separate pieces of cardboard. Cover them with clear contact paper so they'll last. The baby can play "cards," by matching each picture with it's twin.

The baby's books should always be available to him. He may want to read to himself, and he'll sit and point out all the things he sees in his books.

Cut out and mount pictures of foods that the baby is familiar with. Let him look at these and practice naming them. Two children would probably help each other here, since one would name what the other couldn't. This would be a learning experience for both, but you should be there to help them when they get stuck.

Put a collection of small toys or objects in a box, and let the baby name each toy as you get it out.

Take the baby out for a walk and point out all of the things that he sees. Maybe he will be able to point at and name some of the things for you.

All of the babies will have a good time picking their own pictures out from the pictures of all of them. They may point to the pictures of the other children and say their names. Here again, they can learn from each other.

When you read to the baby, read slowly. This gives the baby a chance to look at the pictures, and to point to the things he knows or is interested in. Try letting the baby set the pace by letting him turn the pages. If he starts to turn from back to front or skip pages, maybe he just wants to look at and name pictures. This is alright too.

142

The baby is learning how to ask for what he wants now. Sometimes he may point to something as if he were asking for it. When he does, give him the name of the article in a sentence. Encourage him to say it also. If he can't manage the whole sentence, see if he will say just the name of the article.

One thing the baby will be looking for from you is praise for his efforts. We have been encouraging you to continually praise him, but don't go overboard here either. You don't want the child to feel he has to have praise and approval for every little thing he does. He may come to be overly dependent on your approval. It is important for the baby to begin to develop confidence in his own judgements. Remember, a little praise goes a long way. In fact, the baby himself will soon be aware of false praise, and "turn you off."

The baby is finding out, with your help, how powerful words are. He can begin to control his world when he can use language to help him.

The baby may seem to overdo his word power sometimes, especially when he discovers the strength of "no." It's your job to help the baby manage his language in a way that brings satisfaction to himself and is also acceptable to you and other people.

Help the baby to ask for things by placing two or three of his favorite toys out of his reach. Tell him their names, using a complete sentence. Encourage him to say the name of the toy, and reward his efforts by giving him the toy he asked for. A word of warning here: don't tease or frustrate the baby. If he cannot or does not want to say the word you're after, let him have the toy to play with, and try again another time. If the baby seems to be confused when he tries to say what he wants, help him. Say something like, "This is your milk, and this is your cookie." Let him try to say the words, then give him what he asks for. Use caution again here so as not to frustrate him.

You probably know the baby and his needs so well that you can tell what he wants before he asks for it. However, you should give the baby a chance to ask for it first. He will never get a chance to use or find out the effectiveness of language if he gets everything he needs without having to ask for it.

For instance, if he shows you an empty mug, don't just fill it automatically. Ask the baby to tell you what he wants, and give him a chance to answer, even if he can only get out the word "milk." The important thing is to keep the baby talking.

You may notice something that the baby will do to help himself learn and remember words. This is when the baby goes on and on in a parrot-like way, saying things over and over. This is called "echolalia." He'll sound something like this: "Tommy want cookie?", "Want a cookie," "Here's a cookie," "This a cookie," and so forth. Don't be disturbed by this. It is normal for this age, and does help the baby to practice words.

143

The baby will learn how to use "manners" words like "Thank you," and "Please" if you are careful about using them when you talk to him and to other people in the center. Make a good model for him to follow.

Preaching to the baby about "company" manners probably won't work. He needs to see you and other adults practicing good manners all the time, and not just for company. Then the baby will learn to express his friendly feelings, as you do, all the time in a natural way.

When the baby learns what to do and say in any social situation, he will be able to gain respect and approval from others. Children who have not learned these social responses will be uncomfortable about themselves in their future life in school and elsewhere. They'll know that they are not doing something "right," and will begin to have bad feelings about themselves. Help the baby to avoid this by starting him on the right path as soon as you can. Show him by doing. Practice what you preach.

Play a "Please and Thank You" game with the baby. Give him a small toy and then ask for it back, saying "please" to him. If he gives it to you, then say "thank you." The baby will think this is fun and will probably want to keep it up. Playing this way with the baby helps him learn "manner" words, so that he can begin saying them himself.

Here are a couple of rhymes to help you teach the baby about "manners" words:

> Baby got his teddy bear,
> The magic word was "please,"
> If he says "thank you," also,
> He'll get a hug and squeeze.
>
> Hello, everybody so merry and gay.
> We're happy to see everybody today.
> We'll sing, and we'll dance, and then we'll play.
> Then we'll all say "goodbye" and go away.

144

The baby is busy learning new words, new language every minute of his day. One way he adds new words is by asking questions. It will seem to you that he's constantly asking "What's that?"

Try to answer as many of the baby's questions as possible. You can help the baby learn even if you let him touch or point to the objects as you name them for him. Encourage him to try to say the name after you.

Another thing you can do while helping the baby name things is to let him make some choices. This is a skill also, that must be practiced to be learned.

You can ask him whether he would like a chocolate or vanilla cookie, for instance. Encourage him to use words to answer you, rather than just pointing, even if he only reaches and says, "Cookie." At first the baby may not understand, but as time goes along and you keep giving the child choices, he will be able to make choices on his own.

It's particularly good to name words in connection with activities for the baby. For instance, if you are helping the baby wash his hands, tell him that he is "washing," that he is using "water," that "water" is "wet." All the things that you and the baby do each day have names, and the baby will learn better if he can connect these names with his actions. Learning words this way helps the baby understand ideas and learn to think.

Learning words in this natural way will also help to cut down on some of those "What's that?" questions. The baby will be using you as a resource to learn new things and new words. You won't be able to devote all of your time to just the questions of one child. It won't hurt for the baby to learn that there is a limit to the amount of time you can spend answering his questions. Just tell him that you can't answer any more questions now because you have something else you must do. It won't hurt to tell him what it is you are going to do. Babies understand quite a bit. This is how they learn about compromise and cooperation.

The important thing is to talk to the baby and answer his questions, as many of them as you can, within reasonable limits. The learning of language is a major accomplishment of the baby's second year. It's your job to help him by talking to him, naming things and actions, and encouraging him to talk and learn.

The baby can now understand more things that you say to him, and can say more things himself. He now can begin listening to more complicated sentences and try to use them himself.

One way to get the baby started on longer sentences is to start giving him two part directions. Give him things that you know he can do. For instance, say "Dennis, get your truck and put it in the toy box." He may pick up the truck, but then forget what to do with it. Gently remind him again by saying, "Put your truck in the toy box." You may have to go back to giving just one-step directions again, but remember to try two-step directions during all of your daily activities with the baby.

A good game to help the baby learn is to cut out many pictures of objects. Then ask the baby to pick out the picture you name and put it in a box or paper bag. Say such things as "Pick out the dog, Sonya, and put it in the box," or "Jose, can you find the picture of the truck and put it in the box?" You can play this game with small toys also.

Another way to play is to cut out pictures of objects and ask the baby, "Pick out the picture of the spoon and put it with a real spoon." You may find that the baby will understand better at first if he is asked to put the object into something.

In any case, if the baby seems not to like these games, or if they seem too hard for him, stop and try again a few weeks later. Don't try to push him if he is not ready.

As you begin using these two-part sentences, you'll find that the baby will also become more independent and begin to use longer, more adult-like sentences. But at this age, the child's pronounciation and speech rhythm are not yet under control. He may also speak loudly because his voice control is not yet at an adult level. He may start to speak, then stumble over his words, stop, and start again. But don't worry; the baby is still learning and he is probably not going to be a stutterer or use slow or halting speech forever. Just be patient with the baby, and don't call attention to his problems in speaking. If you do, he may think that you disapprove of his efforts, and stop trying.

You have to remember that with children's speech, their temperament is important. Some children chatter all the time, while others like to be quiet and watch. Some children start to try out words much sooner than others. However, by the time the baby is two or three years of age, he will be using speech quite freely.

Remember also, that children talk more frequently if they have something to talk about. Be sure to give them things to talk about by giving them plenty of interesting activities to take part in. Sand and water play, finger painting, outdoor play, walks, visits to nearby places of interest, such as the park, the fire house, other centers, and so on will all give the children many things to talk about, and so inspire their use of speech.

APPLE TREE ACADEMIES, INC.
PO BOX 4206
GREENSBORO, NC 27404

Another game you can play is the "Directions Game." This is a game where you give the baby directions he can follow, such as "Sit down...Stand up...Go to the window...Crawl under the chair," etc. You can also play a game where you begin a story and then ask the baby, "What do you think will happen now?" or "What if this happened?" Let the baby think up his own answers, and even finish the story if he can. A good story beginning might be "Tara's father just finished baking a cake...," then ask the baby what happens next. You can think of many story beginnings that will be simple yet interesting for the baby, and the baby will be able to think of a lot of story endings.

146

Make language important to the baby by responding, listening and above all, by encouraging him. His desire to talk may be turned off if nobody bothers to talk to him or listen to what he says. This is especially important as the baby goes through what you might call the "chatterbox" stage. He will keep on adding new words to his vocabulary all through his life, but never will the rate be as great as now.

Puppets are toys that are especially good for language development. When you put a puppet on your hand and talk to the baby "through the puppet," you'll be surprised at the reaction you'll get. The baby will really "talk" to the puppet, and not realize that the voice is coming from you. You can get a lot of interesting insights about the baby's speech and the baby in general when he "talks" to a puppet. Make the puppet have a funny voice, and make funny sounds. The baby will love to repeat and play with these funny sounds. Nonsense sounds with a good rhythm will also delight the baby, and he'll try to say them too. Along with having fun, the baby is also learning to "get his tongue around" various sounds that are necessary for good speech. Here are some examples:

> Gaggle, gaggle, gaggle, glop,
> Sing a little song for pop.
> Guzzle, guzzle, guzzle, goo.
> Sing another song for you.
>
> The airplane has such great big wings,
> And as it flies it always sings,
> Up we go, vroom-vroom-vroom,
> Down we come, zoom-zoom-zoom."

Tick, tock, tick, tock,
The mouse ran up
The big brown clock.

Tock, tick, tock, tick,
That was just a
Small, brown mouse trick."
(Say each line in the rhythm of a slow clock ticking.)

The baby is ready now for short stories. Before you may have been spending more time just pointing to and naming pictures. Read to him now as often as you can. Keep the stories and pictures simple. Let the baby point out pictures he recognizes, but he may now be more interested in the story itself. Talk about the stories during other parts of the day with the baby. You can say something like "Come on, Tara, we're going to play like the little girl in the book." You'll find that you'll be reading favorite stories over and over again, because they are what the baby likes to hear.

Toy telephones are valuable in encouraging the baby to use his speech. Talk to the child, and let him talk to you. Let the children talk to each other on the telephone also. Once you get them started doing this they'll probably take over and do it often on their own, since their imaginative play is also beginning to come out. A walkie-talkie *(see #140)* will also be useful for encouraging the baby's speech. A tape recorder is another way for the baby to learn by hearing his own speech, and the speech of other children and adults he knows.

When you are reading to the baby, encourage him to interrupt you and talk about whatever he wants to talk about. He may see something that reminds him of something else, and he may even talk about it. It may be something he wouldn't want to bring up directly. For instance, he may see a big dog that he says is scared. This lets you know that he notices and is interested in talking about being scared. You can say, "Yes, that dog was scared. I bet you're scared sometimes, too. I know I am." In this way you can help the baby talk about and lay to rest worries he may have. Remember, the baby's worries may seem small to you, but they are very large to him.

Play and sing with recordings, or just use your own voice. The children will not worry about whether you sound like an opera star. The important thing is that they have a chance to sing and dance for a short time every day. These kinds of activities are good for the "whole" child—for his language development, for his physical development, for his emotional and social development, and for his intellectual development. This is also one of the best ways to work with children in a group.

You probably know all of the old favorite nursery songs. But it is a good idea to play, sing and dance to music of other cultures. If you have Hispanic children in your class, try to get some Hispanic folk dances, tunes and rhythms. Try the "Mexican Hat Dance," or play mariachi records so the children can dance to them.

If you know the song "John Henry," sing it or play it. Two records that are good for black culture are *American Negro Folk Songs and Work Songs and Rhythms*, and *Negro Folk Songs for Young Children*. Both of these records are by Folkway Record Corporation. All of Ella Jenkins records are also good. Try the record *Rhythms in Nature*, also by Folkway Record Corporation.

The children will enjoy it if you tape record with them as they sing together. Then they can sing and dance to their own music. You may even have one who will do a solo for you.

Don't forget to provide the children with rhythm instruments to play with the music, such as triangles, bells, sandpaper blocks, etc. You can have fun letting the children try to imitate the noises that the instruments make. Let them try to imitate other noises such as a siren, a truck, etc. Music time is a good time to teach the children about soft, loud, high, low, etc. Sing songs loudly, then softly, and then let the children try it.

A fun game to do with music is the "Loud or Soft Game." Let one child "hide" a large object, such as a teddy bear, somewhere in the room. Make sure it's in plain sight. While the child is "hiding" the toy, take another child out of the room until it is hidden. Then this child can walk around looking for the toy, while you and the other children sing loudly when he gets near and softly when he is far away. Be sure to explain this to the child who is doing the hunting.

Here's a rhyme that will be helpful for singing softly and loudly:

(Soft voices)   Leaves are floating softly down.
                     They make a carpet on the ground.
(Loud voices)   When swish, the wind comes whirling by,
                     And sends them dancing to the sky.

Make some picture cards for the baby by pasting or drawing simple pictures on 4″ by 6″ cards. Have one side of the card show the front of the object and the other side show the back of it. Make sure they are familiar objects like an adult woman (Mommy), a child, or an animal such as a dog. Use objects that are not alike also. Make some of the picture cards so that they match exactly (front and back) and make others different.

You can let the baby play with the picture cards and see if he can find the ones that match exactly. Another way to use them is for you and the baby to look in a magazine and see if he can "match" one of his cards with a picture in a magazine. When you play this game, at first use only one card for the baby to match. He may later become good enough to hold two or three cards and match them all with pictures that look like them in a magazine.

Blocks can be used for sorting and matching in many ways. At first, you should let the baby play with the blocks his own way. He'll handle them, inspect them carefully, play with them and try to build things with them.

You can help him learn while he plays if you'll talk with him and show him that there are little blocks and big blocks. It's better at first if you only use two sizes of blocks that are all of the same color. Ask him to give you one size and then the other until you've built something and the blocks are all used up. When the baby gets good with two sizes of blocks, you can use a jumbled pile of three or four sizes and shapes. Ask the baby to hand you one like the one you have. Help him to understand size by running his finger over the edges, and by letting him look at it from all angles. When he picks a block to match it, compare it by holding the edges of the blocks together. Ask him if he thinks that it matches. Use your imagination and creativity to get across the idea of "alike," or "matching." As you and he decide that the block matches, put it in one pile. Go on playing matching games until all the various sizes are in separate piles. If the baby seems unhappy or frustrated with this game, don't force him to go on with it. Just let him play with the blocks in his own way. Remember in all of these games to use words that describe, such as small, large, long, short, etc.

Blocks can also be used for matching colors. For this, begin with only two sets of colors, such as a set of red blocks, and a set of blue blocks. The blocks should all be the same size. Then see if the baby can match the color with another just like it. Say the color names. The baby most likely will not be able to tell you the color names. Don't expect this, or expect him to hand you a block when you name the color. Just help the baby to find matching blocks. Go through the whole group of blocks until you have sorted them into piles of different colors.

When using these kinds of sorting and matching games, remember that the baby can only remember one fact about an object at a time. So make sure all the items used in the game are the same in every way but the one you are teaching the baby. For instance, if you are sorting for color, the items should be exactly the same size and shape.

If you cut action pictures from a magazine or coloring book, you can help the baby learn the meaning of actions and the names of the actions. Ask the baby what the person in the picture is doing. If he doesn't know, you can tell him, and then ask him again. Always use full sentences when you speak to the baby, and encourage him to use them too. You can do this by taking the baby's words and answering him by using them in a sentence. For instance, if he looks at the picture and sees a man mowing the lawn, he may say "man" or "Daddy." Then you can answer him by saying, "Yes, Daddy (or the man) is mowing the lawn." Encourage the child to say this about the picture.

All throughout the day you should be using the baby's words in sentences for him to hear and perhaps say himself. A good time for this is lunch time. If the baby reaches and says "carrot," you can say, "Yes, Louise, I'll give you a carrot." Keep doing this kind of speech building as often as you can. Don't correct the baby however, or make him feel that he's wrong. Just re-use his words as you answer him.

Another way you can help the baby associate words with actions is to make a scrap book for him. On one page paste a chair, and on the other page paste a chair with someone sitting on it. You can make a whole book of these kind of pictures, using objects such as a stove, a telephone, and other things that the baby is familiar with. You and he can have a good time looking and talking about what things are used for.

The baby can also use this type of object/activity matching pictures if you'll mount them on 4″ by 6″ cards. Let the baby match the object with the activity it is involved with.

Use these picture cards with the baby by letting the baby imitate the action that is shown, also. Let the baby pretend to be cooking, sweeping, or talking on the phone, etc. Let him pick out the card he wants to imitate himself.

Sometimes you can use real objects with the baby, and ask him what it does or is used for. You might try showing the baby a cup, a broom, a cake of soap and so forth. Use your imagination and above all, use your voice—talk to the baby in full sentences.

Teach the baby to plan with words when you and he are doing a puzzle. Say, "Here's the piece that goes at the top," and "Let's turn this piece around until we can see if it fits." This helps the baby to make things clearer to himself as he solves a problem. When he learns to talk about a problem he is solving, you can ask him to whisper. Much later, he will be able to say it to himself silently. Talking about the problem is a good problem-solving strategy that you are teaching the baby.

A good song for learning to match words with actions is "This is the Way We Wash Our Clothes" (also known as "Here We Go 'Round the Mulberry Bush"). You can make up some of your actions for this same tune. It's a good idea to teach the baby the name and use of unusual objects that he may not see very much. Carpentry tools are ones that the baby may not be familiar with. Tell him their names and show what they do. For instance, say "This is a hammer, and this is a nail, Martha. Watch while I hammer the nail into this wood."

One of the first things that the baby should know about himself, after his name, is how old he is. Teach the baby how old he is by holding up and counting your fingers and saying his age aloud. Soon he will be holding up the right number of fingers and saying his age, as he has seen and heard you do. Make sure that he knows that this is the answer to the question, "How old are you?"

Play a sorting game with the baby. To begin with, use just two sets of objects that are exactly the same except for one feature, such as color, size, etc. If you are using blocks, for instance, show the baby that you want him to put all of the red blocks in one box and all of the green blocks in another box. While he is doing this with you, talk about him taking one red block from the pile. Tell him that the pile has many blocks. After he has taken one block, ask him to get another block. The baby needs to learn the ideas of one, of many, of another, and so on.

In connection with this, the baby should also know about plurals. Demonstrate for him saying "Here is one red block, and these are many green blocks." Hold up your fingers and say, "Here are all of my fingers," and "This is one finger." Show him how to do this with his own fingers. You can play a good game with the baby by letting him hold up one finger or all of his fingers while you tell him how many you see. He'll have a lot of fun even if he can't count the number of fingers yet.

All day long you'll find opportunities to talk about one and many, using singular and plural words. These are basic math concepts that the baby needs to know before he can go on to later math skills.

Don't forget when you're talking to the baby that he must also learn about past and future tenses of verbs. Let him learn about such words as "today," "tomorrow," and "yesterday." Use them as you talk to him. Show him the calendar. Look at the clock. Talk about what you did yesterday or will do tomorrow, as in "Guess what, children? Tomorrow we are going to make play-dough."

Give the baby other skills that he will need for later school success. Try stringing beads with him. Put on a blue bead for instance, and then let him find another "just like" yours and put it on the string himself, with you helping. Pretty soon you and the baby will be able to try two strings, with the baby putting beads on his first, and you putting on ones that match his. Sometimes, for fun, make a "mistake" and see if the baby notices. As you are working with the baby, keep talking about colors, shapes and concepts of "one," "another," etc. Bead stringing provides practice for writing, drawing, and basic counting skills. The baby will enjoy playing with bead stringing on his own. Let him do it as often as he chooses, and he will choose it often. Listen closely and you may hear the child telling himself to put "another bead" and "another bead" and so on. Now you know he is learning.

Let the baby look out the window at the people and traffic going by. Hold him, or let him stand on a low stool. Talk to him about what you see. Say things like, "There goes a red truck," and "Here comes another truck," or "Look at the two girls skipping," and "Those three boys going in that house are brothers." The baby will be interested and soon start to tell you what he has seen. Encourage him. Say "Yes, Joey, I do see that big brown dog," or "That is a lot of children running by." Use many descriptive words, use plurals, and use many other kinds of words. The baby is learning how to speak from you.

A good way to teach basic language and math skills is to cook something with the children. They are not too young now to understand and enjoy what you are doing. Use a very simple recipe, perhaps one that just requires mixing if you don't want to use heat around the children. One that the children will enjoy making and playing with after it's made is play-dough. Talk about what you are doing. Count "how many" out loud as you measure the ingredients. Give everybody a chance to knead it or to mix it. Let the children try this with spoons and with their hands. Which way do they think is better?

Some good recipes to use with children can be found in Vicki Lanski's book, *"Feed Me! I'm Yours" (see bibliography)*. One good recipe is her "Play-Dough Ala Peanut Butter." You'll find it on page 94 of the book. It's a mixture of peanut butter and honey, with non-fat milk added (or flour) to make it the consistency of play-dough.

150

Now the baby's imagination is coming into play more and more. He probably has already pretended to feed his teddy bear or rock it to sleep. Imaginative play or fantasy provides many opportunities for the baby to exercise his language skills. Encourage this.

One of the best ways to encourage imaginative play is to let the children play "House." Set up the "Housekeeping Center" with plenty of "props" besides the usual stove, sink, table, and so on. Give the children much food for imagination. If you can get parts of uniforms, such as a police officer's or firefighter's hat, or a nurses's cap, the children can act out these roles. Use your imagination and provide as many props as you can think of. You don't have to put them all out at once. Changing the items from week to week makes it all the more interesting for the children. Provide as many different kinds of cooking and eating utensils and other household items as you can. You can use adult-size utensils, as long as they are safe for the children to play with. For instance, a large egg-beater, or a sieve is fine, but stay away from large knives and forks. Plastic spoons and child sets of silverware and dishes are better. Adult size plastic dishes and containers are alright.

One of the best things about this kind of "housekeeping" play is the immense amount of language use and learning that takes place. This happens when you are talking to the children and encouraging them in their "pretend" games, and also when they talk and interact with each other. Then too, this is one of the best settings for young children to learn how to play with each other, as a step to growing away from parallel play.

Books and magazines provide exercise for the baby's imagination. Let him look at and talk about things he sees. Encourage him to imagine what will happen next, and to make a "story" about the pictures he sees. You can also use picture cards or toys for the baby to play "pretend" with. He can pretend that the kitty is sleeping, or that the teddy bear is crying, and so on. Much of this imaginative play is good for the baby. It helps him get rid of worries and fears by his "imaginings." You'll be able to notice the things that he "pretends" that the doll or other object is doing, and recognize the problems or worries he has. Let him play them out. Talk to him about them by entering into his pretend play with him.

You'll notice that as the baby talks to his toys and dolls, he'll speak to them the way adults speak to him. You might even recognize yourself. Then you can decide whether you are providing a good model for the baby to follow.

Puppets are an excellent way to provide imaginative play for the baby. You can make simple finger puppets, or sock puppets for the hand. It doesn't have to be an elaborate puppet. The baby will love to play with it anyway.

Toy telephones, blocks, trucks, dolls, doll houses, and doll furniture are all good for encouraging the imagination. Outdoors you can have "trikes," scooters, and wagons. The children can pretend to be truck drivers, bus drivers or all sorts of things. Don't forget to have a filling station. Children love to pretend to "fill-er-up" and pay for the gas, get change and so on. The sandbox and its activities provide the source for much "pretend." So does water play or blowing bubbles.

Indoors or out, it's fun to set up a store. Many learning areas open up here, giving much language experience.

Read some simple poetry for the children, and then let them "imagine" about it. Dance can also be expressively imaginative. Let the children pretend to be snowflakes, the wind, animals, and so on. Use your imagination. Play music that has no vocal accompaniment. Then let the children use their imagination to tell and dance how it makes them feel.

151

When the baby cries, you know that he's telling you he is dissatisfied or uncomfortable in some way. Your job is to find out why, and then do something about it. Try to be always aware of all the babies you care for so that you can prevent problems from occurring as often as possible. One of the most common causes of the baby's crying is hunger. The baby will also cry if he feels lonely or neglected. You should see that they both are filled and so keep crying at a minimum. There is always a cause when the baby cries, and you will probably be able to figure it out and do something about it as soon as you can. The important thing is not to let the baby cry for very long periods without trying to do something for him.

Since the health and safety of all of the babies is in your hands, you should always make a point of thoroughly washing your hands after every diapering, after using the bathroom yourself, and before feeding the baby. Careful and regular hand washing is perhaps the most important precaution you can take to safeguard the health of the children in your care. Remember also to watch out for small objects that the baby could swallow or put in his ear, eye or nose. Be sure all such objects are out of the baby's reach, especially when diapering him.

For good crib safety, always keep the side rails up and securely locked in position. Remember that deep pillows or loose materials, particularly plastic bags, in the crib with the baby can suffocate him. Remove anything in the baby's crib that could stop him from breathing immediately. Knot plastic bags before you discard them. Then if the baby somehow gets one, it will not be as harmful. If you see any child playing with a plastic bag, get it away from him quickly.

The baby's own temperament plays a big part in whether he cries readily or not. Some babies will put up with a lot before they cry, and others let out a yell at the least sign of hunger or discomfort. As you get to know the babies in your care, you'll find this out, and be able to care for the babies better.

Consistency is one of the most important things you can give the baby. He needs a small number of the same people to relate to day to day so he can develop basic trust and confidence in "his people" and in himself. That's why it's important that you work with the same babies every day.

152

Even if the baby is able to drink from a cup, he may also still need to be treated as an infant on occasion. It may make him feel more secure to sit in your lap while you hold him in your arms. Let him hold his own bottle, but give him the chance to be "cozy" with you while he drinks it. Try to keep it a private time together. Don't let other children bother or annoy the baby while he drinks his bottle.

Other babies may not need or want to sit on your lap while they take a bottle. They'll fuss and let you know they are not happy. The child like this may do better if he's left to drink his bottle on his own. However, don't be surprised if this child sees how much others enjoy their "happy time" with you, and insists on his turn. All babies need to be cuddled, after all.

"Propping" the bottle for the very young baby may be necessary once in a while, but try to do this as little as possible. When you prop up the bottle for the baby to drink from, you deprive him of that warm, secure, and comforting feeling of being held in your arms. It forces the baby to rely only on himself when he is eating. It makes meal time a "cold" time for him, and you may find that it will make him want to hold on to drinking from a bottle longer than necessary. This is because the bottle itself is the only source of comfort he gets when he is is always left alone to eat. In order to make it possible for you to hold the baby as he takes his bottle, first make sure that the other babies in your charge are made dry and comfortable. Provide them with something interesting to watch or a favorite toy. Then you can settle down with one baby while he takes his bottle.

153

Encourage the baby when he begins to try to feed himself. This helps the child get a feeling of independence. It also is an excellent way for him to develop small motor skills in using his hands. It may seem sometimes that it's easier for you to feed him, because he will be messy as he tries to feed himself. Remember though, that if you continue to feed him you are not letting the baby develop either independence or motor skills and control.

Provide the baby with finger foods that he can easily pick up. At first, he will only be able to pick them up in his fist, but soon he will be able to use his thumb and forefinger in a pincher grip. Show him how to eat finger foods by doing it yourself. If he can't do it himself, try taking his hand and showing him how. The baby will probably be reaching for the food all by himself as soon as you put it out. Make sure the food is easily chewable and digestible for the baby. Don't give him small hard foods, such as any kind of nuts, because he can too easily choke on them. Popcorn or raisins are not good for babies under two years either. Other foods that may cause the baby to choke are the strings in celery or string beans.

Give the baby food that is easy for him to handle. This way he won't get tired, cranky and awkward because he cannot handle the food as well as he would like to. Some good finger foods are large crackers or pretzels, bits of bread or toast, or bits of cheese or meat. You can make it a lot easier for yourself if you only give the baby one to two pieces of finger food at a time. If you give him more, he might stuff everything in at once and then choke. He might also sweep everything onto the floor.

At snack time leave the baby to himself as he eats his finger foods. You can do something else and just be "around" in the room, so that you can easily replace his food as he eats it. He may spend as much as an hour picking up bits of food, examining them, putting them in and out of his mouth, etc. Let him, since this is a good learning activity for him.

The baby will eat more of his finger food at regular meal time if you give them to him first. Then he will be hungry, and will complete much of his meal with the nutritious and delicious finger foods you serve him. Let the baby look at himself in the mirror as he eats. This will fascinate him as he watches his mouth chewing.

154

Put just a few drops of milk or juice in the bottom of the cup when the baby is first learning. Increase the amount as the baby becomes better at it. At first you can hold the cup for him, and then maybe both of you can hold it together. However, the baby is an independent little person, and he will soon want to hold the cup for himself. Encourage him to, even if he spills quite a lot in the beginning.

Let the baby hold his empty cup while you are feeding him. This way he can learn how to pick it up and put it down. It is important for him to learn this so he can do it later without spilling. In fact, you can also let the baby play with his cup when he is not eating. Then he can get acquainted with it and learn how to handle it without interfering with your feeding him. Demonstrate the way you pick up a cup, drink from it, and put it down again. Then let him try. Let him watch in the mirror as you and he do this. He'll be even more inspired to try to do it like you do. If the baby shows signs of reluctance to use the cup, don't insist. Some babies seem to be more dependent than others, and cannot adjust to new ways so quickly. They seem to like being fed and as long as they indicate this, you should feed them. Soon enough they will begin to feel independent enough to try for themselves.

You should always remember to use an unbreakable plastic or metal cup for the baby. It should not be too big, but of a size that the baby can easily hold in both hands.

Give the baby a spoon to hold while you are feeding him. He'll have one of his hands occupied as you try to feed him and his other hand will be busy with his finger foods. As he sees what you do with the spoon, he soon will be trying to imitate you and do it himself.

Pretend once in a while to take a spoonful of his food yourself. See what the baby does then. Don't tease him, though. The baby learns from watching and imitating your actions, so always demonstrate actions that you want him to follow. Sit behind the baby as you feed him and let him hold on to the spoon or your hand. This is a good way for him to learn the motions of self-feeding. Of course, this method will slow you down and be considerably messier, but remember, it's teaching him.

As the baby begins eating solid foods, he might seem to lose interest in food, and even eat less. He may also refuse a food he has always liked. He may eat a certain food at one time and not at another. Don't worry about this, because the baby's rapid growth begins to slow down toward the end of his first year. He needs less food in proportion to his body size now, so this is normal for him.

Give the baby foods that are easy to handle and make sure he is not tired before he begins a meal. If he is tired he won't try to feed himself for very long. If he still seems hungry, but unwilling to feed himself, you should feed him, and maybe the next time he'll do better. If the baby has trouble holding the spoon, try wrapping some tape around it to give him a better grip.

It's fun to pretend to eat at a "tea party" with the baby. This is one more way to show the baby how to handle spoons and other items we use to eat with.

When the baby is first learning to use his spoon, give him foods that are easily managed. Good foods to use are thick oatmeal, pudding, or mashed potatoes.

Make sure the baby is comfortable as he sits to eat. Be sure the table is the right height for him, that his chair is comfortable, and that he has plenty of room to move his arm. You should always make sure the baby is in an upright position when he is eating. When the baby has finished eating, let him play and practice for a while with his empty dish, spoon and cup.

156

The baby can learn by putting objects into containers. Start with large objects in even larger containers, then work down to small objects in large containers, and finally small objects in small containers.

Save all of the clean and safe containers of every shape and size that you can find. Bring them into the center so the baby has a variety of things to put things in. These containers will fit into each other also, and give the baby more ways to play with them.

Play a fetching game with the baby. Give him practice in picking things up by asking him to go get a block for you, or to bring you a spoon, and so forth. He'll gets lots of practice picking things up for you. He'll learn also that he is being useful to you, and this will make him feel good. Squeeze toys that make a noise when picked up will help the baby to be interested. Doughnut-shaped toys or objects are easier for the baby's little hands to pick up than solid toys or objects. Balls or tubes are also good. Make sure that the objects used are not small enough for a baby to swallow. Small objects that are edible, such as finger foods, are also good practice for the baby. Try Cheerios or pieces of Zwieback. Drop them on a clean piece of plastic or paper on the table or the floor and let the baby try to pick them up *(See Activity #14).*

157

Make things as easy as you can for the baby. If his hat has a button, unbutton it, but let the baby take the hat off himself. When he sits down to try to take his shoes off, help him here too. Untie or unbuckle the shoes so he can pull them off. Don't be too surprised, however, if the baby beats you to it by pulling his shoes off while they are still fastened.

Put a hat on your own head and let the baby take it off and put it on. He will love this game. Talk about what the baby has achieved. Make a remark like "Why, James, you took my hat off all by yourself. Good for you."

Play some games with the baby as you help him undress. Try playing "Peek-a-boo" with the hat he has just taken off. He'll enjoy this, and will soon start doing it himself. Sing a song while you help him.

Try making undressing time a pleasant and happy experience for the baby. Help him learn to help himself. Allow plenty of time; you don't want the baby to feel rushed. Let him do as much as he can or will for himself.

Don't expect the baby at this age to do more about undressing himself than dealing with very easily removed items, like his hat or shoes. Remember too, that his parents may have gotten them for that very reason. The important thing is to encourage the baby to do what he can without making him feel badly about what he cannot do.

Try not to keep the baby cooped up so that he has no place to walk around in while he explores his world. When the baby starts to walk, his world opens up for him if he is given the chance to walk around and investigate. Just be sure that you have a "child-proof" area for him to walk in—an area where he will be safe from harm, but that still has many stimulating objects that he can use the way he wants.

Many pull toys and things the baby can push or drag after himself are good for encouraging the baby to walk. Show him what happens when you pull something on a string. Then let him do it—he'll be anxious to do it for himself. Ask him to go get things for you. He'll enjoy being an errand runner and feel good when you thank him for bringing an item to you. Be sure to give only one clear direction at a time. Otherwise the baby will get confused and frustrated. Make sure he knows how to do what you ask him to do. Can he find the diaper pile and reach it safely, if you ask him to bring you a diaper, for instance?

You'll find that the baby is much more active, and seems to have more energy now that he can walk and get around on his own. He'll be more independent, and perhaps a little bit bossy. This is because he has found a thrilling new world, and can do some things in it for himself. He can fetch things for himself and others, for instance, and so is beginning to be able to control his world. You are faced with the problem now of how much you can let him do and still keep him safe. The baby is now at a crossroads in his life and needs your constant supervision and reassurance that he can do for himself, while feeling secure in the knowledge that you are always there to help and encourage him.

The age that each individual baby begins to walk depends on many things. It depends on the baby's temperament. How cautious is he? Is he courageous enough to try to walk? His body weight and build have an effect also on when he'll begin to walk. Many other things, such as his physical health and the freedom he's had at the crawling stage also have an effect.

Here's something very important that you may have already found out. You won't be able to teach the baby to walk until he's ready. And when he's ready, you'll find it next to impossible to stop him. You can help develop good walking and standing posture by setting an example yourself of good posture.

Here are some other things that result in good posture. Try to help the baby get them:
1. Good nutrition
2. Plenty of fresh air and exercise
3. Naps taken on a firm flat cot
4. Plenty of rest after illness
5. Happy and wholesome center atmosphere, where the baby feels loved and secure—then he'll be confident enough to practice walking.

When the baby is first learning to walk, you can put a small chair on its front side. Let the baby push it in front of him as he tries to walk. The legs make handy "handle bars" for him to hang on to as he pushes the chair and staggers along after it.

When the baby can walk fairly well, give him something to hold as he walks. As he gains control of this skill, let him try a toy for each hand. Work your way up with the sizes and weights of the things you give him as he walks.

159

The baby is growing more independent, and you may think, also more demanding. Every time you can answer one of his requests the way he wants it, you are helping to increase his self-confidence. There is no way, however, that you can give him everything he wants. You can help the baby to make reasonable demands if you try to respond to the ones that are reasonable, and tell him "No," *and mean it*, when he is being unreasonable.

Remember that the baby is trying to learn how far his power goes, and will really use up a lot of energy while doing so. He's testing what things he can and cannot expect from you. It's up to you to help him learn this.

Help the baby learn how to use words, phrases, and eventually sentences to ask for things. If you give him what he wants when he is just reaching for it, or making baby sounds, he will never speak for himself. When he reaches for his cup, for example, say "Oh, Kevin, do you want the cup? Here's a nice cup of milk." Sometimes, if you know that the baby knows the word, ask him to say the name of the item before you hand it to him. If you always ask the baby for things by name, and name articles for him as he uses them, you'll soon teach him that all things have names. Pretty soon he'll be asking for things by their names.

The baby and you spend a lot of time together during the day. If you play a game of asking him for something, and then let him ask you for something, he'll learn the way to ask for things. Just make sure he knows the names of the articles you are working with. For instance, say "Maxine, can you give me the dolly?," and when the baby does, you can then say "Now, what do you want me to give you?" Help the baby to select and name a toy that he wants you to give him.

Play a game with two or three children by having them pass toys back and forth to one another. For instance, you can hand one child a ball, and then say to another "Denise, ask Pablo for the ball." Encourage him to use his own words to ask for what he wants. Then give another child a chance to ask for the ball.

The baby probably has already begin to take part in undressing himself. Among the first things he can do are to pull off his socks, hat and mittens. He also can put out his arm or his leg for a sleeve or pants to put on. As the baby does these things, talk to him about what he is doing. You can encourage and reward him if you say things like "Look at Danny, he pulled off his hat and mittens all by himself." Show him you appreciate what he does.

You can put large adult socks and other clothes in a "dress-up" bag, and the baby will get a lot of practice in dressing himself. Help him if he needs it, but encourage him to try for himself first.

Talk to the baby as he is being undressed or dressed. Tell him about what you and he are doing together. Say "Now, Lorene, we'll pull up these socks; you help me," or "Push your foot into your pants leg, Marvin. Make your foot come out the other end." Talking and doing at the same time reinforces what the baby is learning about dressing himself. Here's a little song you can sing with the baby as you help him get dressed.

> Put your little sock,
> Put your little sock,
> Put your little sock right on,
> Put your little shoe,
> Put your little shoe,
> Put your little shoe right on.
> *(Sing this to the tune of "Put Your Little Foot Right Out.")*

Gradually the baby will begin to dress himself, with you giving things a helping hand along the way.

Simple, easy-to-put-on clothes are the key to making it possible for the baby to begin helping himself to dress or undress. Of course, you cannot control this, but try to tactfully encourage parents not to put the baby into clothes that are complicated and difficult to put on or take off.

Let the baby take his coat or shirt off himself after you have unbuttoned or unzipped it. He'll probably be proud to learn this, and you'll be helping him to feel more self-confident and independent.

161

When you are dressing the baby, he is going to be interested in helping you. Let him help you all he can, but don't expect him to be able to pull up his own zippers on clothes he is wearing. He needs to practice on other zippers first.

Make a dress or jacket for a large doll and put a large zipper in it. Then the baby and you can dress the doll together. When you get to the zipper, hold the material taut and let the baby try to pull the zipper up.

If the baby has trouble trying to get a hold on the zipper tab, put a handle made from a pipe cleaner or a notebook ring on it.

You can make a zipper board if you tack the front of an old jacket to a piece of plywood. Make sure the tacks are securely hammered in and don't let the baby play with this board unless you are with him.

162

The baby is beginning to notice that he is uncomfortable with wet or soiled diapers, and will start letting you know about it. Praise him when he lets you know, because this is a sign that he is beginning to be aware of his body functions. This is a big first step in toilet training.

Did you know that through your facial expressions and other silent cues, the baby can tell how you feel about his soiling himself? Don't let him know that you are displeased or disappointed in him; try to be matter-of-fact about changing him.

The baby is probably beginning to have regular bowel movements. Make a note of the baby's bowel movements and wetting patterns, so that you can begin to help him get to the toilet before he soils himself. The baby should be willing to go to the bathroom with you; this shows that he has a vague idea of what it's all about. However, if he is balky or won't cooperate, and cries when you try to "catch" him, stop and try again a week or two later. He probably wasn't as ready as you thought he was.

Now the baby may be arriving at the stage where toilet training can begin. Try to have a talk with the baby's parents about this so that you can coordinate your efforts with their methods of training. It's important to be consistent with the children, particularly in this area. Use the words that the baby has been taught at home for his bodily functions.

One way to help the baby to get started is to let him sit for a short period (no more than five minutes), on a child-sized baby seat on the toilet or on the potty chair. Make sure that the seat is comfortable and secure. It is important for the child to feel secure and confident. Do this at regular intervals during the day. He will probably void or have a bowel movement while sitting on the potty at some time during the day. If he does, praise him and reward him immediately. A hug and a kiss may be enough. Give him the association of using the toilet and having a pleasant experience. This way he'll want to repeat his performances. Remember that good toilet habits are complicated to learn, and good timing on both your part and the child's part are important.

While the baby is still this young, don't concentrate on anything more than getting him accustomed to sitting on the potty, so he can learn what it's for and how it is used. Stay with him, talk to him while he is sitting on it, and if nothing has happened, just matter-of-factly take him off it. Allow him to help you pull up his pants.

164

Take advantage of the baby's eagerness to learn, and let him try to wash and dry his own hands. At first he will want to spend time just playing with the soap and water, and you should try to humor him in this. Soon he will learn from watching you that "big people" don't play in the water when they wash their hands. Try to always set a good example for the baby. Remember, he must learn to wash his hands every time he uses the bathroom. You can help him learn if you will begin by washing and drying your own hands while he is watching, so he can see exactly what to do.

Now you can help the baby to do all of the steps involved by "talking" him through them in an encouraging way. Say "Good for you, Reginald, you got your hands so nice and clean!" Work through the entire process step-by-step by letting the baby do one thing for himself, and then adding another step until he can do the whole process by himself. Just make sure he can do one step before adding another. For example, he should be able to soap his hands well before he proceeds to the step of rinsing and drying.

Pretty soon you'll find that you can just tell the baby to wash his hands without your having to take part or hover over him. Don't forget to let the baby know the reason that it is important for him to wash his hands. Keep it on his level, though. Say "Washing hands is good fun, isn't it, Noah? And it's good for you, too. We want you to be a healthy boy."

165

By this time, the baby should be able to tell what is edible and what isn't. He should have learned about this from you, because you have always been careful to tell him what is not for eating.

Now he can be encouraged to be independent, and feed himself as much as he can. This is particularly important for a child of an independent nature. In fact, you'll probably find that he will refuse to eat if you try to feed him. He may still spill things on the way to his mouth, but he'll learn if he's allowed to practice on his own.

If you have used the various suggestions offered in *Activities #153, 154,* and *155,* the baby may be coping with eating quite well by now.

Sometimes the baby may be feeling unhappy or "low," so he may revert to babyish habits and want you to feed him. This is where it's important for you to know the child. Does he really need a little bit of cuddling today? Then it's alright for you to help him, but if it becomes a habit, you should realize what the baby is doing and try to discourage it.

166

The baby is becoming more and more independent, and dressing himself is a good way for him to express his independence. He can probably undress himself even more rapidly than he can dress himself. Let him do this too, but at the proper time. Unfortunately, you may find that the baby will undress himself at other times, also. He likes to show how much he can do and how independent he is. If the baby does undress himself at the wrong time, you can turn it into a learning experience by asking him to help you put the things back on again. Challenge him to try for himself.

Help the baby learn how to put on a dress or pants by going through the steps involved and talking about them as you do them. Gradually let the baby do more and more of the steps for himself. Say things like "Hold up your arms, LaDonna, and we'll pull your dress down over your head. Good! Now let's slip your arm in this sleeve." If you tell the baby and show the baby how at the same time you are giving good learning reinforcement. Allow the baby to dress himself as much as he can. He may get something inside out or backwards, but he is also getting a great feeling of satisfaction since it was done all by himself.

Occasionally the baby might be feeling uncooperative about getting dressed. Say something like "You look so nice in your red shirt, Shelly. How about putting it on for me so I can see you in it?" Maybe this way you can catch the baby's interest, and he'll cooperate after all.

Some other hints for helping the baby learn to dress may be found in *Activities #157, 160,* and *161.*

167

The baby wants to please you, because he identifies with you. If he sees you doing something, he will want to do it too, because he wants to copy what you, a grown-up, can do. Then he'll see that doing things like you brings him rewards in the form of pats and hugs, and finally inward satisfaction because he has pleased you.

Make it easy for the baby by showing him how to pick up toys, and where the toys go. Sing a little song if you want to, while you are doing this, and encourage him to help you and sing along with you. One song you might use is "Now it's time to pick up your toys," to the tune of "Here We Go 'Round the Mulberry Bush."

To make it even easier for the baby to participate in putting toys away, be sure they are kept on a low shelf or in a box that the baby can easily reach. You could put pictures of the toys on the shelves or boxes, so the baby will know where the different kinds belong.

Name or describe the different toys as they are picked up. Say "Here's the red dump truck, we keep that right here." Then suit your actions to your words by putting the toy where it belongs. Next time encourage the baby to put it where it belongs. Say "My goodness, Tamika, you certainly know where the red dump truck goes, don't you?" in a pleased voice.

When clean-up time is coming, give the children advance notice that it's time to clean up. They may be ready to stop playing sooner if they know that you'll soon be asking them to clean up their toys.

If you plan something interesting or important for the children after clean-up, they'll be anxious to get ready for it. Say something like "After we get cleaned up, we are all going for a walk." Giving the children something pleasant to look forward to acts as a stimulus.

Let the children know why we have to clean up. Say perhaps, "We'll put all of your toys away so we can find them again the next time," or "We need to put our things away so they don't get stepped on and broken."

If you keep all the toys and equipment in the same place all of the time, you'll make it easier for the baby to remember where things go.

168

The baby must be helped to learn to tell you when he needs to use the toilet. Steps that help to get him to this point are described in *Activities #162* and *163*.

Before he can do this, he needs enough muscle control to hold back where previously he just released. At about this age, he should be able to begin to learn, but remember all children are different. Real bowel control can be taught to most children after they learn to walk, so a positive attitude that is rewarding to the child should help him to learn. Try to remember that without pressure from you, the child will slowly but surely make the change from wetness to dryness.

Ask the baby's parents to cooperate by dressing him in clothes that are easy to take off. Simple pants with elastic waistbands are much better than overalls that go over the shoulder. Now is also the time to ask the parents to put the baby in training pants rather than a diaper.

Try to follow the baby's own rhythm, which you should now be familiar with. Try to "catch" him when you know it's the usual time for him to need the bathroom.

When you think he needs it, lead the baby gently and calmly into the bathroom. Remember, he should be used to sitting on the toilet by now. Help him with pulling down his outer pants and his training pants. Take his hand and let him help you to push them down. Be pleasant and smiling, and say something like "Here goes Randy, up on the toilet seat." Stay with him, and when he achieves, reward him with a smile and a hug. It's important to make using the toilet a good, happy experience for the baby. Wipe him carefully when he has finished, and help him down gently. If he wants to help you wipe or flush, let him, but be sure he is clean. Then let him help you pull up his clothes.

All of the time you are with the baby in the bathroom, talk to him about the sounds and smells. Assure him that they are natural, and that what he produces is something he no longer needs, so now he can get rid of it. Make it a positive experience for the baby.

Don't forget good health habits. Make sure the baby's hands are washed after he uses the toilet, so he gets into the habit of knowing that this is what he must always do. He'll probably enjoy using soap and water, so try not to hurry him.

169

Now that the baby is over his second birthday, he'll really show progress in dressing himself. It will be up to you to see that he has all of the time he needs to dress himself. You'll still have to finish up things for him, like tying his shoes, and so forth. He'll probably also still need help in getting zippers started, or the little top button undone, or the snap snapped.

As the baby is able to do more and more things for himself, while dressing or undressing, notice where he cannot do something but still seems to want to try. This is the time to try teaching him the more difficult dressing skills, such as buttoning and unbuttoning. Be sure to teach him only one skill at a time. Help him learn to unbutton, for instance, before teaching him to button.

Teach every new skill in a step-by-step fashion. Show the baby the first step, and then let him try it. Don't rush him, and if he seems to be getting frustrated, leave it until another time.

Something fun to do while the baby is learning to dress himself is the "discover" game. As the baby puts on his coat, for instance, say things like "Where's Rodney's hand?" This will encourage him to pop it out of his sleeve and laugh happily as you then say, "Why, here it is." Do this with other steps in dressing or undressing. Make it a fun time for the baby and for you.

Many other suggestions for helping the baby learn to dress will be found in *Activities #157, 160, 161,* and *166.*

170

To help the baby feed himself, try always to use a child-sized spoon with a short handle. The use of a bowl rather than a flat plate will also help the baby, because he'll be able to push his food against the side of it. This will help him get the food onto the spoon rather than onto the floor.

Check to make sure that the baby is seated comfortably. Are his elbows just above the level of the table? Are his feet flat on the floor? Is his back well supported?

Some of the suggestions in *Activities #153, 154, 155,* and *165* may still be useful, even though the baby has progressed beyond the beginning stages of learning to eat and drink.

171

Up till now you have probably been helping the children to put away their toys. But try to just ask the children to put away their toys themselves. Challenge them. Say, for instance, "I bet you boys and girls can't put all of these toys away without me helping you." With some children, you might find it works better to say something like "Children, can you give me a big hand today and put away your toys? I have something else I must do."

Of course, the children will not always feel like putting the toys away, but if you remember to give them something to look forward to after the toys are away, you'll get much more cooperation.

Activity #167 offers other ideas for helping children learn to clean up.

172

Helping the baby to learn how to get his own drink will make life easier for you, and the more the baby can learn to do for himself, the better it is for his self-confidence and growing independence.

Teach the baby how to do this task, as others, in a series of simple steps. The first thing to make sure of is that the baby can easily reach a cup and the spigot. Place a low stool in front of the sink, so the baby doesn't have to climb. The steps in getting a drink of water are: 1) get a cup, 2) turn on the spigot, 3) hold the cup under the stream of water until it is as full as required, 4) turn off the spigot, 5) drink from the cup, 6) pour any left over water back into the sink, 7) discard cup (or put it where it should go to be washed.)

Let the baby watch you as you get a drink. Then get him one. Let him help you as you again go through these steps. You'll find that steps 5, 6, and 7 are the ones he'll first be able to do by himself. Work back gradually from step five to step one, letting him try one more step each time. Soon he'll be able to do all of the steps himself. Be sure that the baby can get a drink easily before you stop going to help him. Perhaps the baby will be very independent, and will tell you he can get his own drink and you don't have to help him. Make sure he can, and then let him.

The baby is probably completely toilet-trained by now, and is probably also very proud of it. You should be proud, too, since you have played a large part in his successful training.

You have respected his readiness, rather than forcing your schedule on him, and now he can take himself to the bathroom, and do almost everything for himself, with only a little help from you. The baby will feel more secure if you are with him in the bathroom. Accompany him if he wants you to, and keep a pleasant conversation going. As he sees other children using the bathroom on their own, he'll gain confidence, and won't need you any longer.

It's important however, that the baby learns how to use toilet tissue properly, and remembers to always wash his hands afterwards. Teach him how to use toilet tissue by holding his hand and guiding it, so that he understands what to do. For a while some not too obvious supervision on your part should help the baby to remember these very important health habits.

It's very important that you act warm and supportive of the baby if he has an "accident." Don't make him feel ashamed or tell him he is a "bad boy or girl" when he does make a mistake. His self-confidence about handling body functions is only starting to build, and you don't want to break it down again. Sometimes a child really can't help it when he has an "accident." Don't assume that he's doing it just to be naughty.

Another thing to remember through the toilet training period is that the early or late achievement of complete toilet training has absolutely no bearing on mental or physical excellence. Each child is different in all development, and each should be valued for himself and what he can do.

BIBLIOGRAPHY

American Speech and Hearing Association. *Partners in Language: A Guide for Parents.* Washington, D.C.: Staff Project; The Prevention of Speech and Language Handicaps, 1973.

Anderson, Andrew L. and Washington, Esther M. *The Young Child: Ages and Stages of Growth.* (Extension Bulletin #393.) New Brunswick, New Jersey: Cooperative Extension Service, College of Agriculture and Environmental Science, Rutgers University.

Black Child Development Institute, Inc. *Curriculum Approaches from a Black Perspective.* Atlanta, Georgia: A Workshop Sponsored by Black Child Development Institute, Inc., 1973.

Brazelton, T. Berry, M.D. *Infants and Mothers.* New York: Dell Publishing Co., 1969.

Brazelton, T. Berry, M.D. *Toddlers and Parents.* New York: Dell Publishing Co., 1974.

Camden Public Schools. *A Curriculum Guide for Teachers of Kindergarten.* Camden, New Jersey: Division of Curriculum and Instruction, 1966.

Cazden, Courtney B., Ed. *Language in Early Childhood Education.* Washington, D.C.: National Association for the Education of Young Children, 1975.

Chapel Hill Training - Outreach Project, Anne R. Sanford, Director. *Learning Activities for the Young Handicapped Child.* Winston-Salem, North Carolina: Kaplan Press, 1976.

Cherry Hill Public Schools. *A Curriculum Guide for Kindergarten.* Cherry Hill, New Jersey: Kindergarten Curriculum Study Committee, 1969.

Cohen, Monroe D., Ed. *Understanding and Nurturing Infant Development.* Washington, D.C.: Association for Childhood Education International, 1976.

Comer, James P., M.D., and Poussaint, Alvin F., M.D. *Black Child Care.* New York: Pocket Books, A Division of Simon and Schuster, 1975.

Croft, Doreen J. and Hess, Robert D. *An Activities Handbook for Teachers of Young Children.* Boston: Houghton Mifflin Co., 1972.

Dittman, Laura L. *Your Child From 1 to 6.* Washington, D.C.: U.S. Department of Health, Education and Welfare, Office of Child Development, Children's Bureau, 1973.

Dittman, Laura L., Ed. *The Infants We Care For.* Washington, D.C.: National Association for the Education of Young Children, 1973.

Dittman, Laura L. *What We Can Learn From Infants.* Washington, D.C.: National Association for the Education of Young Children, 1970.

Donahue, Mike, et al. *Manual I: Behavioral Developmental Profile.* Marshalltown, Iowa: Department of Special Education.

Earle, Patty T. *A Guide to Early Speech and Language Development for Day Care Teachers of Infants and Toddlers from Birth to Three Years.* Greensboro, North Carolina: North Carolina Training Center for Infant-Toddler Care, The University of North Carolina, 1976.

Furfey, Paul Hanly, Ed. *Education of Children Aged One to Three: A Curriculum Manual.* Washington, D.C.: The Catholic University of America, School of Education, Curriculum Development Center, 1972.

Gesell, Arnold, M.D., et al. *Infant and Child in the Culture of Today.* New York: Harper and Row, 1943.

Gordon, Ira J. *Baby Learning Through Baby Play.* New York: St. Martin's Press, 1970.

Gordon, Ira J. *Child Learning Through Child Play.* New York: St. Martin's Press, 1972.

Griffin, Patricia M., and Sanford, Anne R., Director, Chapel Hill Training - Outreach Project. *Learning Accomplishment Profile for Infants (LAP-I).* Winston-Salem, North Carolina: Kaplan Press, 1975.

Group Care of Infants and Toddlers: A Demonstration Project. *Assuring Safety and Protecting Health.* Greensboro, North Carolina: University of North Carolina.

Harrison-Ross, Phyllis, M.D., and Wyden, Barbara. *The Black Child.* New York: Berkeley Medallion Books, 1973.

Huntington, Dorothy S., Ph.D., et al. *Day Care 2: Serving Infants.* Washington, D.C.: U.S. Department of Health, Education, and Welfare, Office of Child Development. (DHEW Publications #(OCD) 73-14.)

Ilg, Frances L., M.D., and Ames, Louise Bates, Ph.D. *Child Behavior.* New York: Dell Publishing Co., Inc., 1955.

Keister, Mary Elizabeth, Ph.D. *'The Good Life' for Infants and Toddlers: Group Care of Infants.* Washington, D.C.: National Association for the Education of Young Children, 1973.

Lanski, Vicki. *Feed Me! I'm Yours.* Wayzata, Minnesota: Meadowbrook Press, 1976.

Lischner, Kyong, et al. *Developmental Play as a Learning Tool: Birth to Three Years.* Glassboro, New Jersey: Bozarth Early Childhood Demonstration Center, Glassboro State College.

Mussen, Paul Henry, et al. *Child Development and Personality,* Third Edition. New York: Harper & Row, 1969.

National Institute of Neurological Disease and Stroke, Information Office. *Learning to Talk: Speech, Hearing and Language Problems in the Preschool Child.* Bethesda, Maryland: National Institute of Health, 1969.

North, Frederick A., M.D. *Infant Care.* Washington, D.C.: U.S. Department of Health, Education, and Welfare, Office of Child Development, Children's Bureau, 1973.

Parent Training Program. *Toilet Training* (a leaflet). Pitman, New Jersey: Educational Improvement Center. (As adapted from an article by Molly C. Gorelick, California State University, Northridge).

Sanford, Anne R., Director, Chapel Hill Training - Outreach Project. *Learning Accomplishment Profile (LAP).* Winston-Salem, North Carolina: Kaplan School Supply Corp.

Saunders, Minta M. *The ABC's of Learning in Infancy.* Greensboro, North Carolina: The Infant Care Project, University of North Carolina, 1971.

Schirmer, Gene J., Ph.D., Ed. *Performance Objectives for Preschool Children.* Sioux Falls, South Dakota: Adapt Press, Inc., 1974.

Segal, Marilyn, Ph.D. *From Birth to One Year.* Fort Lauderdale, Florida: Institute for Child Centered Education, Nova University, 1974.

Segal, Marilyn M., Ph.D. and Adcock, Don. *From One to Two Years.* Fort Lauderdale, Florida: The Nova University Play and Learn Program.

Southeastern Day Care Project. *Evaluating Children's Progress: A Rating Scale for Children in Day Care.* Atlanta, Georgia: Southern Regional Education Board, 1973.

Tronick, Edward and Greenfield, Patricia Marks. *Infant Curriculum: The Bromley - Heath Guide to the Care of Infants in Groups.* New York: Media Projects, Inc., 1973.

Spodek, Bernard, et al. *A Black Studies Curriculum for Early Childhood Education: Teaching Units.* Urbana, Illinois: ERIC Clearinghouse on Early Childhood Education, 1976.

Upchurch, Beverly. *Easy-To-Do Toys and Activities for Infants and Toddlers.* Greensboro, North Carolina: Infant Care Project, The University of North Carolina, 1971.

Willis, Anne and Ricciutti, Henry. *A Good Beginning for Babies.* Washington, D.C.: National Association for the Education of Young Children, 1975.